Praise for De-

What a read! At the end of the day, ch ...id
making sure that no matter what our congregation size is, we engage with the culture
and community around us. Thank you, Karl, for the reminder. I'll be recommending
this book to pastors everywhere.

GREG ATKINSON, author, speaker, founder & CEO of the First Impressions
Conference and EntreChurch

In *De-sizing the Church*, author Karl Vaters alerts us to the dangers of a "bigger is
better" mentality in life and ministry. Without "throwing the baby out with the
bathwater," he analyzes the historical development of popular church growth thinking in the United States, offering insightful analysis and helpful critique. He argues
for a balanced appreciation of all sizes of churches, while calling church leaders to
use integrity as their core measurement of success rather than numerical growth.
Whatever your viewpoint regarding the health and growth of churches, *De-sizing
the Church* is worth the read!

GARY L. MCINTOSH, Distinguished Professor of Christian Ministry & Leadership, Talbot School of Theology, Biola University

Karl Vaters single-handedly changed the conversation on church size in America.
Tracing the trends and trenches the church growth movement fell into, Vaters now
hands us a shovel to dig our way out. A timely book that will rescue you from the
fads, and lead you back to the facts—timeless facts that are principled from the
pages of Scripture.

PEYTON JONES, cofounder and CEO NewBreed Training; author of *Church
Plantology*

De-sizing the Church is a ministry-changer—refreshing, liberating, and transforming!
For over forty years of pastoral ministry, I felt an unrelenting pressure to produce
numerical growth. My emotions and sense of worth cycled up and down with the
weekend attendance. Chasing the wind is exhausting. Rediscover what matters most
in ministry in *De-sizing the Church*.

DAVE BECKWITH, Standing Stone Ministry, and author of *God Meetings*

De-sizing the Church is the right book at the right time! As always Karl Vaters puts
into words what many of us are feeling but struggle to express. His ability to confront
the problem without becoming just another a church critic is both refreshing and en-
lightening. Whether you pastor a church that runs 50, 25, 500, or 1000+ on a Sunday
morning this is a must-read. Thank you, Karl, for your consistent kingdom impact!

MICHAEL J. RUBINO, founder of the Church Revitalize Center

The expectation that every church will grow is a major factor in clergy burnout. In *De-sizing the Church*, Karl Vaters has provided an antidote to that poisonous belief. He demonstrates how the obsession with bigness has compromised our faithfulness and what we must do to recover healthy ministry.

SEAN NEMECEK, Regional Director for PIR Ministries and author of *The Weary Leaders Guide to Burnout*

In *De-sizing the Church*, Karl Vaters challenges the American belief that "bigger is better," especially regarding church size. In my spiritually formative years, small was better for me, as I was raised, saved, and called to the ministry in a small rural Virginia church with ninety attendees. I encourage you to read and heed this book's message to value the church and its pastors through heaven's eyes. Let us cherish every church and its pastor(s), regardless of size, who faithfully and effectively carry out biblical Great Commission ministry.

TOM HARRIS, President, Interim Pastor Ministries

For far too long church leaders have been operating under age-old paradigms about church growth without even thinking about where they originated. In *De-sizing the Church*, Karl Vaters pulls back the curtain on these almost universally accepted practices, and then challenges and empowers church leaders to realign their thinking with true biblical models.

CRAIG T. OWENS, author of *Shepherd Leadership: The Metrics That Really Matter*

I am convinced that Karl Vaters is the voice that the American church needs at this moment. A lover of the local church, he is calling us to do healthy, sustainable ministry, regardless of size. *De-sizing the Church* is a practical call to set aside our obsession with bigness and instead focus on creating disciples of Jesus who faithfully and healthily engage the world around us.

MATT STEEN, cofounder, Chemistry Staffing

De-sizing the Church is a cautionary tale of what goes wrong in ministry when we confuse numbers with calling. Vaters has written an *autopsy of the Church Growth Movement*, helping us to see where it got sick, and why we need to get better at telling the difference between our culture and the gospel. If the question "How big is your church?" makes you wince, you'll find comfort here along with encouragement to bear down on discipleship and to put the yardstick away.

RICK HIEMSTRA, Director of The Evangelical Fellowship of Canada's Centre for Research on Church and Faith

Karl Vaters delves into the church growth movement with a pastoral heart and a consultant's eye and challenges us to rethink our obsession with metrics. He urges pastors to elevate stories over stats and refocus on ancient yet new priorities as we seek to grow healthy churches.

JOHN FINKELDE, founder of Grow a Healthy Church

DE-

HOW
CHURCH
GROWTH
BECAME
A SCIENCE,
THEN AN
OBSESSION,
AND WHAT'S NEXT

SIZING
THE CHURCH

KARL VATERS

MOODY PUBLISHERS
CHICAGO

All Scripture quotations, unless otherwise indicated, are taken from the Holy Bible, New International Version®, NIV®. Copyright ©1973, 1978, 1984, 2011 by Biblica, Inc.™ Used by permission of Zondervan. All rights reserved worldwide. www.zondervan.com The "NIV" and "New International Version" are trademarks registered in the United States Patent and Trademark Office by Biblica, Inc.™

Scripture quotations marked (ESV) are from the ESV® Bible (The Holy Bible, English Standard Version®), © 2001 by Crossway, a publishing ministry of Good News Publishers. Used by permission. All rights reserved. The ESV text may not be quoted in any publication made available to the public by a Creative Commons license. The ESV may not be translated in whole or in part into any other language.

Scripture quotations marked (NKJV) are from the New King James Version®. Copyright © 1982 by Thomas Nelson. Used by permission. All rights reserved.

All emphasis in Scripture has been added.

Edited by Amanda Cleary Eastep
Interior design: Ragont Design
Cover design: Erik Peterson
Author photo: George Samuel Beaver

Library of Congress Cataloging-in-Publication Data

Names: Vaters, Karl, author.
Title: Desizing the church : how bigness became an obsession, why it
  matters, and what to do about it / Karl Vaters.
Description: Chicago, IL : Moody Publishers, 2024. | Includes
  bibliographical references. | Summary: "We thought bigger was better.
  "Church growth" and "numbers" dominated our thoughts and conversations.
  But more than ever, people are feeling disconnected. Vaters invites us
  to consider how removing church size from the equation can be an
  essential element in rebuilding trust, restoring relationships, and
  renewing our spiritual lives"-- Provided by publisher.
Identifiers: LCCN 2023039058 (print) | LCCN 2023039059 (ebook) | ISBN
  9780802424259 (paperback) | ISBN 9780802499875 (ebook)
Subjects: LCSH: Big churches. | Church management. | BISAC: RELIGION /
  Christian Living / Leadership & Mentoring | RELIGION / Leadership
Classification: LCC BV637.9 .V36 2024 (print) | LCC BV637.9 (ebook) | DDC
  254.0068--dc23/eng/20231016
LC record available at https://lccn.loc.gov/2023039058
LC ebook record available at https://lccn.loc.gov/2023039059

Originally delivered by fleets of horse-drawn wagons, the affordable paperbacks from D. L. Moody's publishing house resourced the church and served everyday people. Now, after more than 125 years of publishing and ministry, Moody Publishers' mission remains the same—even if our delivery systems have changed a bit. For more information on other books (and resources) created from a biblical perspective, go to www.moodypublishers.com or write to:

Moody Publishers
820 N. LaSalle Boulevard
Chicago, IL 60610

1 3 5 7 9 10 8 6 4 2

Printed in the United States of America

Dedicated to the memory of my grandfather, Eugene Vaters—
a man of integrity and a pastor to pastors

.

Contents

Preface

De-sizing
[de-**siz**-ing]
verb

1. The process of assessing the value of something without obsessing over numbers.

2. In the church, choosing to evaluate the health and vitality of a congregation, a denomination, or a movement without using attendance figures, percentages, or numerical comparisons as the primary consideration.

Introduction

*For the Christian leader, there should be only one
metric that matters: faithfulness.*

Tim Suttle

Numbers define us. They shouldn't, but they do.

- "She has 5,000 social media followers."
- "He makes $20,000 more a year than I do."
- "That church runs 3,300 people on five campuses."
- "Our church only has 40 members."

Numbers aren't bad, of course. Tracking my 10,000-steps-per-day count has motivated me to stay healthier. But numbers are meant to inform us, not define us.

So, why do we define ourselves by numbers so regularly? And how have numbers become the default way that so many pastors and churches perceive our value in the kingdom of God? Followers of Jesus should not perceive their value or identity in terms of numbers. In Christ's upside-down kingdom, the first will be last and the humble will be exalted. Yet, for my entire four-plus decades in ministry, the answer to the question "What's your church running?" has been the primary way pastors have defined themselves, their congregation, other churches, their sense of identity, and their value.

And it's killing us. Literally and metaphorically.

Our obsession, not just with numbers, but with big numbers,

may be the major—but least-acknowledged—contributing factor in pastoral burnout, church scandals, divisiveness, misallocation of resources, and many other church dysfunctions. As Darvin Wallis sadly but accurately notes, "The moral failures of church leadership are not anomalies. They are the norm because they are baked right into the corporate leadership paradigms the church has embraced."[1]

Church size matters to us far more than it should. From the pride it brings when the numbers are up to the shame and frustration it causes when the numbers are static or down, none of this provides a healthy foundation on which to build a healthy church body.

We need to de-size the church.

Church growth is not the problem. Big churches are not the problem. *Bigness* is the problem. Bigness is an obsessive mindset. Bigness convinces us that more is always better. Bigness hides character flaws beneath numerical success. Bigness is a disease that creates *dis-ease* in everything it touches and everyone within its orbit.

We have an unhealthy relationship with bigness in the church, especially in the American evangelical church and in countries that have been heavily influenced by it. This book is not anti-American or anti-evangelical. I *am* an American and an evangelical, but I am a follower of Jesus first. That is what forms my identity and my ideas ahead of everything else.

I have yet to meet a highly driven, spotlight-chasing, crowd-pleasing church leader who doesn't believe they are keeping that drive alive in order to truly reach people for Jesus. No doubt there are scam artists who use Christian language and imagery to squeeze money out of people. They get the headlines, but they aren't nearly as common as cynics think. Most of us are fighting a Romans 7 battle with varying degrees of success, trying to reach people for Jesus while the constant gravitational pull toward pride, fame, and compromise tugs at our weakest points.

But how did we get here? How did bigness become such an

obsession that many good pastors constantly feel overwhelmed by the pressure to get the numbers up? The drive to succeed has always been there, of course. The desire to work, to build, and to create is hardwired into us as carriers of the image of our Creator-God. But ever since Eve's conversation with a pesky little serpent, that innate, God-given yearning has become twisted. It's no longer enough to build and create as a reflection of the glory of God. Our fallen humanity demands that the glory reflects on us. And there's no quicker way to feel the warm glow of that reflected glory than seeing the numbers go up on attendance charts and financial reports.

The idea of a church constantly getting bigger began as an outlier. Then it became a goal. Now it is the standard by which the performance of all churches is measured. Our obsession with numerical success is overwhelming pastors, stifling churches, and ruining our witness. Size comes at a price. There's a price to get to it, a price to maintain it, and a huge price when it doesn't work out as expected.

This is why we need to de-size the church.

What Is De-Sizing?

De-sizing is a new term. I coined it because new ideas need new words to express them. De-sizing is not up-sizing. It's not downsizing. It's not even right-sizing since there is no "right" size. De-sizing is about rethinking our approach to church size and numbers until attendance, finances, and percentages are no longer the primary factors we use to assess a local church's calling or effectiveness. In some cases, they won't be a factor at all.

De-sizing is not thinking that big churches are bad—they're not. It's also not wanting churches to be smaller. De-sizing is not a refusal to look at or learn from numbers. Numbers are a normal and necessary part of life and health. But they can't be the primary lens through which we see the health and effectiveness of a church body.

You are not your numbers. Neither is the church you serve.

The church's mission is bigger than numbers.

De-sizing *is* about disconnecting our sense of value from our size. De-sizing is about getting off the relentless, Sisyphean treadmill of rolling that boulder up one hill today, only to roll it up again tomorrow. Numbers need to be used in the right way. To inform us, not define us. Stop chasing the next numerical goal of attendance, finances, online engagement—all of it. You are not your numbers. Neither is the church you serve.

In the debate over church size there are three primary opinions:

1. bigger is better
2. smaller is better, or
3. size doesn't matter

I propose a fourth option—neither bigger nor smaller is better, but church size does matter. However, it doesn't matter in the way we think it does. Church size matters the way shoe size matters. It's not about one size being inherently better; it's about finding the right fit.

* * * * *

Sometimes a great idea meets the perfect moment and BAM! everything aligns in such a way that massive crowds show up. This happened a few times in Jesus' ministry, especially as the news of His teaching and miracles grew and He started heading toward what people thought would be a showdown in Jerusalem. But, aside from a handful of extraordinary moments like that, crowds don't happen organically. From the grand cathedrals of old Europe to the shiny new megachurches of today, when we see massive crowds at Christian events it's because a passionate, driven person captured a momentary zeitgeist, then assembled a highly skilled team to pursue it and the crowd with a brilliant, market-driven organizational structure. The numbers don't chase us; we chase the numbers. This is not necessarily wrong. If you have an idea you're passionate about, you'll want as many people as possible to hear it. And, in the case of the gospel of Jesus, we have the best idea ever (far more than an idea, of course), so we should be passionate about getting Christ and His message to as many people as possible. This means utilizing all the tools at our disposal. Or does it? Maybe there are some tools, some strategies, some market-driven concepts so out of sync with the gospel of Jesus that they should never be used in the same breath as the message of the crucified and risen Savior. Methods matter. They shape our understanding of the underlying ideas. And one of those market-driven concepts that we need to strongly reconsider is the church's obsession with size.

Our attitude toward church size affects everything. If you want the church to be small, it will affect the choices you make and how you minister. If you want it to be big, that will have the same impact, but in the opposite direction. Our attitude plays a huge part, often subconsciously and invisibly, in every major decision we make in the church. Wise leaders will drag this often-unspoken factor into the light and into our consciousness. If not, it will keep impacting us in ways we don't realize, and it will continue to hurt churches, their pastors, their members, and our witness to the world.

Smallness is not the antidote to bigness. If bigness is about pride, smallness is about shame. If bigness is about being seen, smallness is about being overlooked. Neither one is healthy, and each will lead down opposite sides of the same dangerous path. The answer is to set aside numerical quantifiers and start seeing our value as Christ sees our value. It's not about how much we have or how little we have, but about who He is, how much He loves us, and the role He calls us to play in the great salvation story He is telling.

Church Growth Arrives, Then Starts to Fade

When I attended Bible college in 1978–1981, there wasn't a single class on church growth, and I don't remember hearing one usage of the term from anyone. Yet within five years of graduating, church growth became the central focus of almost every conversation among pastors and pastoral students. The shift was swift, all-encompassing, and lasted for several decades. The heyday of "Church Growth" (the term) is in the rearview mirror, but its effects linger deep within us, virtually invisibly. Many of those effects are positive; I'm not anti-church growth at all. But the term and the concepts around it have been with us for long enough that we can and should take a clear-eyed look at it.

Church size is a big deal. And a massive industry. Even in books, podcasts, seminars, and articles that don't use the term "church growth," the idea that churches should be getting bigger is embedded in the floorboards. Any church that isn't regularly showing numerical increase is assumed to be "stuck," "plateaued," or "broken" with very little consideration given to the ministry the church may be doing, the impact it may be having, or how its size may be an essential element of its effectiveness.

Three Examples

I really struggled with writing this section. Naming other pastors in a negative light is something I dislike doing. I can't imagine how it would feel if the roles were reversed and someone was writing a book using one of my worst moments as a cautionary tale. But it's important to get specific about how bigness has infiltrated our thinking and to demonstrate why our obsession with bigness is so dangerous. So, here are three examples of pastors: two whose public falls were directly tied to chasing bigness, and one who made a very public and hurtful statement based on an obsession with bigness.

On October 14, 2014, Mark Driscoll resigned from Mars Hill Church amid multiple scandals. Much of his fall has been attributed to arrogance and an extreme lack of accountability. According to several people who were close to him, Driscoll stated that he refused to submit to counsel from anyone whose church was smaller than his, which at the time of his resignation, was almost every pastor in America.[2]

On Sunday, February 28, 2016, Andy Stanley preached a sermon in which he took a short side-route that ruffled a lot of feathers, including mine.

> When I hear adults say, "Well I don't like a big church, I like about 200, I want to be able to know everybody," I say, "You are so stinking selfish. You care nothing about the next generation. . . . You drag your kids to a church they hate, and then they grow up and hate the local church. They go to college, and you pray that there will be a church in the college town that they connect with. And guess what? All those churches are big."[3]

To Stanley's credit, he apologized on Twitter shortly afterward, saying, "The negative reaction to the clip from last weekend's message is entirely justified. Heck, even I was offended by what I said! I apologize." Then he restated that apology in an interview with Ruth Malhotra of *Christianity Today*.[4] I believe and accept that apology. So why bring it up? First, because the damage from the original statement is significant. "It's just one more thing that makes me want to quit," several small-church pastors told me, even after the apology. Second, because it shows how deeply and systemically bigness has infiltrated the mainstream evangelical mindset when small churches can so easily become an unintended target of our frustrations.

In July of 2016, Perry Noble resigned as the pastor of NewSpring Church. In his letter of resignation, he wrote, "*In my obsession to do everything possible to reach 100,000 and beyond*, it has come at a personal cost in my own life and created a strain on my marriage. . . . I began to depend on alcohol for my refuge instead of Jesus and others. I have no excuse. This was wrong and sinful, and I'm truly sorry."[5]

So, in the span of twenty-one months, one pastor quit under pressure after refusing to take counsel from anyone in a smaller church. Another attacked the value of small churches so severely that he needed to apologize immediately and publicly. And a third resigned partly due to what he called an "obsession" with growing his congregation to a bewilderingly large size. Anyone who follows church trends knows that you could pick any recent two-year span and find at least as many similar examples, including thousands of small- and mid-size church pastors who have felt their own church was a failure due to its small size, or who have fallen into moral compromise as they abandoned spiritual and moral depth to chase numerical goals and the fame that accompanies them. Our obsession with numbers has contributed to a host of problems in today's churches, including a lack of discipleship, a watering down of worship, and the replacement of hands-on evangelism with professionalized marketing. I don't believe chasing numbers is the main reason for these problems. But we'd be naïve to think that the constant drumbeat of "more, more, MORE!" hasn't been a contributing factor in the rash of moral failings, toxic leaders, and bodies behind the bus.[6] It has caused too many of us to chase quick answers instead of walking slowly through difficult but rewarding relationships. We reward results even if they come at the cost of our integrity. This has created an untold number of victims and undermined our witness to a watching world.

As pastor David P. Cassidy implored in his Twitter feed after hearing a megachurch pastor tell a roomful of gathered ministers that they shouldn't avoid celebrity, they should seek it, "I'm telling you, platforms are for diving & brands are for horses. Flee from pastors seeking to build them. Leaders tear down with their lack of character what they build with their gifts. Choose humble, faithful, local-focused, word and sacrament serving, people-loving pastors over the polished showmen every day. It might not be sexy, but it won't be toxic and it will be sustainable."[7]

What This Book Is Not

This is not a "What's wrong with the church today?" book, because there is nothing wrong with the church today that hasn't been wrong since the first century. Instead, it's about looking at one specific aspect of today's church that has become a major problem we must deal with.

Our size obsession.

Like no other time in church history, we have become enamored with trying to figure out how to make churches bigger. This book seeks to address a handful of questions that come from this sudden and all-encompassing change, as seen in four main sections, including:

1. "Why is bigness a problem?"
2. "Where did this obsession come from?"
3. "What are the consequences of it?"
4. "What might be a better way forward?"

The answers are not simple. But they do exist.
In this book, I hope to start us on a path to finding them.

Part I

THE PROBLEM OF BIGNESS

Chapter 1

The Danger of
Idolizing Outcomes

*Though we act, and often work hard, it is after
all not our battle, and the outcome is in his
hands. We don't "battle" outcomes.*

DALLAS WILLARD

Before earning my Bible college degree, I spent two years attending
a local junior college. One of my first classes was Economics 101.
The professor began by putting a slide on the screen with a jumble
of words that included *family, faith, job satisfaction, ethics, morality,
fairness, education, wisdom, art, justice, happiness,* and so on. Pointing
at this group of terms (what we now call a *word cloud*) he told us,
"This is what matters in life. Money has an impact on them, but they
are all more important than money."

That's a surprising, but wonderful, start to an economics class, I
thought.

"But that's not what this class will be about," said the teacher as
he removed that slide and replaced it with another. This new slide
had one word on it in huge block letters. MONEY. "That is what this
class will be about," he said, gesturing toward the screen. "For the next

thirteen weeks we will talk about money as if it is the most important thing in life. We will talk about how to make it, spend it, invest it, save it, and more. We will talk as if money is the only thing that matters. But it *isn't* the only thing that matters. The previous slide showed us what matters. Remember that."

That's fair, I thought; *it is an economics class, after all.*

Over the next thirteen weeks, the professor was true to his word. He talked about money as if it was the only thing that matters in life. Then, at the end of the last class, he put the MONEY slide up again. "For thirteen weeks we've talked, read, and tested you as though this was the only thing in the world that matters. I want to remind you that it's not." Then he removed the MONEY slide and replaced it with the original word-cloud slide. "These are what matter in life. Don't forget that. Have a great summer."

I appreciated what the professor was intending to do, but between the first and final class, a huge shift had taken place. On day one, the body language of my classmates affirmed that those were the most important things in life. But thirteen weeks later, their body language was very different. At best, it was apathetic. In many of them, there was a feeling of mockery and disdain—not toward the teacher, but toward the idea that the values on the word cloud were what really mattered. No wonder their attitude toward those values had changed! For thirteen weeks we'd treated money as the *only value* in life. One slide on the screen for a few seconds at the start and end of the semester had no chance of competing with the relentless drumbeat of that message. The word cloud was what we were supposed to pay lip service to so we could see ourselves as members of a polite society. By now we knew better.

In many ways, the last forty-plus years of relentless church growth teaching has felt like that. We've heard constantly about how to increase our attendance numbers. We've been told that this is done in service of the true values of worship, discipleship, ministry, and more. But CHURCH GROWTH is what we talk about *as though numbers are all that matters*, while the word cloud of values increasingly feels like lip service. It's naïve to think that the relentless drumbeat of "How to increase your attendance!" "A proven plan to break growth barriers!" "What you need to know to scale up!" and "Have the faith to 10x your church's impact!" won't overwhelm everything else. Of course, it does.

In *Multipliers*, Todd Wilson indicts the predominant church growth strategies of the last generation. "When a leader's scorecard is rooted in accumulation, he will take his eyes off God and obedience to His commands. Our focus on accumulating more easily becomes a form of *idolatry*, rooted in wrong motives."[1] He later adds that Ed Stetzer and Warren Bird call this pursuit of growth an "*addiction*,"[2] and "the bottom line is that we're facing an epidemic of addition *lust*."[3] Our obsession with numerical addition is "idolatry," "addiction," and "lust." Strong words? Very. Too strong? No. We're obsessed with bigness. Enamored with size. Entranced by churches that keep getting bigger. Worried about churches that don't. But why? Have you ever met anyone who has left the faith saying, "I wanted to serve Jesus, but the church I attended wasn't seeing any numerical growth, so I just couldn't believe anymore"? Numerical growth doesn't impress anyone but pastors and church leaders, and lack of growth doesn't bother anyone but us.

In our skewed approach to church size, we often equate bigger churches with larger faith. In many church growth circles, it's not unusual to hear claims that setting big goals takes big faith, or even that if your goals don't scare you or stretch you, they mustn't be from God. But I have found no biblical basis for it. Not once did Jesus, the apostle Paul, or any early church leader even hint that we should set numerical goals, let alone that setting larger ones would increase our faith. According to Scripture, faith is far more likely to be increased when it's tested through trials (James 1:2–8), when we love one another (2 Thess. 1:3), when we endure persecution (Rev. 2:19; 1 Thess. 3:4–7), and when we lay aside worry and doubt (Matt. 6:28–30; 14:28–31). It's found in trusting Jesus (Matt. 8:10), hearing wise biblical teachers (Heb. 13:7), and seeking God (Heb. 11:6).

Not only is goal setting not in the long list of characteristics that increase faith, but the biblical examples go in the opposite direction. Numerical increase and the trappings of wealth and comfort that come with it are far more often seen as a challenge to faith rather than a means for strengthening it. In Revelation 2 and 3, Jesus criticized the largest, wealthiest, and most prominent churches for leaving their first love (Ephesus), following false prophets (Thyatira), and being lukewarm (Laodicea), while He encouraged the smaller, persecuted churches for remaining faithful to the point of death (Smyrna), despite their trials and limited strength (Philadelphia).

It's not that there isn't correlation between faith and numerical increase. It's that the order of goal setting followed by faith-stretching is backward. While large goals are nowhere seen to increase our faith, sometimes a growing faith does result in numerical increase. In Acts 2, we read that "the Lord added to their number daily those who were being saved," not as a cause of greater faith, but as a result of the apostles' teaching, the breaking of bread, prayers, signs and wonders, giving to those in need, praising God, and meeting together regularly (Acts 2:42–47). We see a similar order of faith followed by blessing in Acts 11:24 where, after Barnabas' arrival in Antioch to assess their theological integrity, "a great number of people were brought to the Lord." Then in Acts 16:5 we see faith first, numbers second, as "the churches were strengthened in the faith and grew daily in numbers."

Goal setting is not the key to growing our faith or increasing the impact of the church. Doing the work of faithful ministry is. Obviously, some goal setting needs to happen. Sermons are due every Sunday, and projects have time-sensitive tasks. But most of the time, ministry is less about setting goals and more about doing good work, one day at a time. The Bible regularly demonstrates this balance with admonitions about how we are to walk in obedience to God, including a wealth of instructions about how to live as the church. And it lauds the wise person for planning, while condemning the foolish one for not preparing.

> Suppose one of you wants to build a tower. Won't you first sit down and estimate the cost to see if you have enough money to complete it? (Luke 14:28)

> Plans fail for lack of counsel, but with many advisers they succeed. (Prov. 15:22)

> On the first day of every week, each of you is to put something aside and store it up, as he may prosper, so that there will be no collecting when I come. (1 Cor. 16:2 ESV)

Planning and preparing are not the same as setting goals and determining outcomes. Outcomes are always in God's hands, not ours.

- In their hearts humans plan their course, but the LORD establishes their steps. (Prov. 16:9)
- Many are the plans in a person's heart, but it is the LORD's purpose that prevails. (Prov. 19:21)
- Come now, you who say, "Today or tomorrow we will go into such and such a town and spend a year there and trade and make a profit"—yet you do not know what tomorrow will bring. What is your life? For you are a mist that appears for a little time and then vanishes. Instead you ought to say, "If the Lord wills, we will live and do this or that." As it is, you boast in your arrogance. All such boasting is evil. (James 4:13–16 ESV)
- I planted, Apollos watered, but God gave the growth. (1 Cor. 3:6 ESV)

We need to stop idolizing outcomes. Let go of chasing after attendance goals, trying to create a buzz, or doing year-to-year comparisons. Just be faithful to the work. Day after day, church service after church service, year after year. When it all adds up, you'll have consistent, faithful ministry that changes lives and honors God.

This is true in every area of life, even in highly competitive arenas where outcomes are considered paramount. For example, Bill Walsh was one of the most innovative and influential American football coaches. He was famous for telling his players that if they focus on the fundamentals, the score will take care of itself. It became so central to his coaching that it's the title of his book *The Score Takes Care of Itself: My Philosophy of Leadership*. If focusing on the fundamentals and not the score works in such a competitive field as the NFL, it should be even more applicable in the kingdom of God, where we're not supposed to keep score at all.

Holocaust survivor Victor Frankl put it this way:

> Don't aim at success—the more you aim at it and make it a target, the more you are going to miss it. For success, like happiness, cannot be pursued; it must ensue, and it only does so as the unintended side-effect of one's dedication to a cause greater than oneself or as the by-product of one's surrender to a person other than oneself.[4]

Church Metrics: Our Three Biggest Mistakes

There are three big mistakes we tend to make with church metrics: overusing them, underusing them, and misusing them.

First, there's a tendency to overuse metrics to assess the health and strength of a church. Relying on numbers as the only way to determine the health and vitality of a church is extremely problematic. The problems show up most obviously in the majority of churches (up to 90 percent) that are regularly referred to as "stuck," simply because their numbers aren't increasing year to year. Many of them *are* stuck, of course. But a lot of them are doing wonderful, missional, kingdom-advancing work that doesn't get the credit it deserves, merely because the numbers don't fit our preconceived ideas. Stuck isn't a number; it's a mindset.

Stuck isn't a number; it's a mindset.

On the other side of the obsession ledger are the churches that seem to be winning at the numbers game. Obviously, many of those churches are doing well, and we can learn from them. But numerical success has pitfalls. When the numbers start going up, the increase feels self-affirming, but soon the need for greater numbers becomes self-perpetuating, and eventually that all-consuming drive can become self-deceiving. It's easy to hide many problems, even outright sins, behind the veil of numerical increase.

When chasing the numbers takes over a pastor's head and heart, it can easily create an obsession that becomes more important than the people and principles that actually matter. This obsession tends to create an alternative reality that the church must wake up from. But we won't wake up easily or without a great deal of pain and disorientation. I believe the church, especially the American church, is in the beginning of that stage right now. We're reeling like a boxer who's taken one too many punches but doesn't know where the pounding is coming from. In many cases, to switch up the metaphor, the call is coming from inside the house.

Second, we mustn't fall into the trap of underusing metrics. Numbers have value. The right metrics can help us keep track of many important aspects of church life and health. Often, they're the canary in the coal mine, alerting us to impending dangers before they become life-threatening. We typically underuse metrics when we assume a church must be healthy simply because it's growing in attendance. A deeper look might uncover warning signs like a corresponding drop in engagement and spiritual maturity. Catching these issues early can help church leaders address them before they eat away at the church's foundation. We'll explore this further when we look at the principle of Goldilocks Metrics in chapter 10.

Third, misusing them. The main way we do this is when we wield numbers as a weapon to exert power and control. This is the problem at the core of everything. The issue isn't really size. It's not even about numbers or metrics. It's about power and control. The pastor of a small church and the pastor of a megachurch are both susceptible to the allure of seizing power and staying in control. And at the root of that is idolatry—taking authority that belongs to God alone.

Chapter 2

When Bigger Is the Enemy of Better

*It's a dangerous and misguided policy to
measure God's blessing by standards of
visible, tangible, material "success."*

KENT AND BARBARA HUGHES

When I was a young man growing up in a pastor's home, there
was a church we regularly attended on vacation. This church
had been in decline for several years. After hiring an energetic new
pastor, it grew quickly. Our next visit was exciting. The place was
packed. It was church membership Sunday, so a couple dozen people
came on stage after having completed the new members' class. This
church hadn't seen that many new members in years, and now they
were growing by that many official members every month, in addition to hundreds of new attenders.

After shaking hands with the new members, the pastor turned
to the congregation and asked, "Would anyone else like to become
a member?" Hands shot up all over the building, maybe a hundred
or more. *Wow,* I naïvely thought, *their next membership class will be
filled beyond capacity!* I assumed the pastor would instruct them to

fill out the "I'd Like to Become a Member" box on the visitor's card. Instead, he told them, "Get out of your seats and come on up here! We'll make all of you members *right now!*" They rushed the stage like shoppers at Walmart on Black Friday.

The pastor prayed over them, shook their hands to welcome them into membership, and sent them back to their seats to massive applause as the band pumped up the music for the next upbeat worship song. I was young, but I knew this was wrong. Instead of two dozen or so new members that morning, their next bulletin (and, no doubt, the report to their denomination) would announce, "Over 100 New Members!" And I had to wonder why the pastor felt the need to inflate the membership numbers that way. He had no idea if the people rushing the stage had ever been in that church before, would ever come back, or even had a relationship with Jesus. Plus, aside from being a dishonest way of inflating numbers, it was entirely unnecessary. Their growth was already enormously successful. It was legitimately the fastest church growth I had ever seen. The extra hype for inflated numbers certainly excited the crowd that day, but it left me feeling empty and sad.

Jesus was already doing something wonderful in that church. There was no need to inflate the membership numbers. That invitation to join the church was not about soul-winning or a passion for lost people. At best, it was about getting caught up in the moment, at worst it may have been about ego. And behavior like this is repeated in churches everywhere, both big and small. The pursuit of bigness is a relentless monster that demands to be fed but will never be satisfied. It consumes everything and everyone in its path.

* * * * *

Howard Schultz, the former Starbucks CEO and the prime figure behind the company's massive growth, said, "Growth covers up a lot of mistakes."[1] He was right. It does. And if you're aiming to please shareholders so they overlook the occasional poor business decision (what Schultz appears to have meant in this context), that may not be a problem. But if you're using numerical success to cover up shallow theology, abusive behavior, or unbridled ego, this is a huge problem, one we've seen far too much of in the church.

Tim Suttle tackles this in his book *Shrink: Faithful Ministry in a Church-Growth Culture*:

> We are going to have to stop our incessant need to make things grow the way we want them to grow, whatever the price. . . . The Christian leader does not pursue success or results the way the CEO of a Fortune 500 company does. The Christian leader pursues faithfulness. . . . I believe that churches that build on the foundation of business leadership principles are building on assumptions that are simply foreign to the gospel.[2]

For decades I was taught that if a church stayed small, it was the sign of a problem. Lack of numerical growth must be due to mission drift, controlling pastors, stubborn members, and so on. That is shifting. Today, the average person is as likely to believe that if a church gets "too big," it's surely the result of greed, theological shallowness, and a consumer-oriented mentality. I reject both presuppositions. Neither the big nor small church is morally or theologically wrong. But it is harder to maintain biblical integrity when a church gets bigger. Size has a pull. And that pull is seldom morally neutral and almost never positive. Wanting to reach people for Jesus and wanting bigger attendance are not the same thing. When we equate them, we get into trouble. I used to believe that pursuing attendance goals was morally positive. It was the fuel for the fire of evangelism. Even after I stopped chasing numbers myself, I saw the pursuit of increased

> **The pursuit of bigness in the church is morally, theologically, and emotionally damaging.**

attendance as a good thing. Today, I still believe there's no qualitative differences between large churches and small ones, but I've heard too many stories of damaged pastors, churches, and members to believe that our obsession for bigger is morally or theologically neutral. So, I'll say it clearly: the pursuit of *bigness* in the church is morally, theologically, and emotionally damaging. Dallas Willard warned us of this, saying, "The need to achieve is too great. Invariably it is the personal and spiritual life of the minister that suffers."[3]

We should prepare for growth. We should be ready for growth. But we should not pursue growth. We should pursue Christ, His mission, His glory, and the making of disciples. It is not possible to pursue Jesus and be obsessed with bigness at the same time without one of them becoming diminished in the process.

Every time we pay attention to numerical increase, we divert some of our time, attention, and energy away from pursuing the glory of God alone. Even when we structure for growth, we should be careful. "Structure is not neutral," warn Dan White Jr. and JR Woodward. In the hierarchical approach to leadership prevalent in US churches and being exported to the world, "the basic measurement of success tends to be counting people, money and the size of the building,"[4] and this way of measuring success has bigger downsides than upsides.

For example, imagine if every time you speak to anyone in a week, you chart it on a graph. At the end of the week, for the pastor of a mid-sized church, it might look something like this:

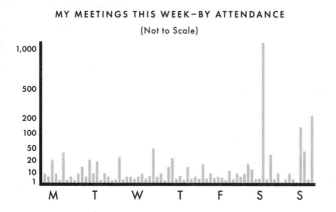

MY MEETINGS THIS WEEK–BY ATTENDANCE
(Not to Scale)

During that week, you had a staff meeting with ten people, conducted a Bible a study with twenty-five people, and held two church services with one hundred and two hundred, respectively. But that week you were also on a panel at a conference attended by a thousand people. If you assess those meetings numerically, the most successful meeting of your week is obvious: the time you spoke to one thousand people wins by a landslide. It might have outnumbered all the other meetings combined.

But take a closer look at the smaller lines. One of them stands for a heart-to-heart talk with your spouse leading the two of you to make a life-altering decision. Another talk was with a couple at the church who reconciled this week, instead of seeking divorce. Several of the four-person meetings were family dinners that imprint long-term habits and memories on the hearts of your children.

Now which meeting is the most important? That answer is impossible. We'll never know the true value of all the ripples from the simplest and smallest encounters. But when we categorize ministries and churches on a numerical graph, we retrain our brain to think that the small meetings are inherently less valuable than big ones. Even though our life experience assures us this isn't true, the constant drive to quantify everything assigns an incomplete, inaccurate, and inappropriate value to the tasks we perform and the people we impact. There's a never-ending line of horror stories about hard driving executives, innovative entrepreneurs, and heavily committed pastors who do exactly that. They sacrifice the small but weighty meetings with the people they *should* be paying more attention to for larger meetings with people whose names they'll never know. By doing so, they're neglecting godly priorities.

The way we obsess over numbers is rewiring our brains and hearts in harmful ways. According to both the Bible and neuroscience, we value what we think about, then we *become* what we think about. We've all seen people who determine that "I will not become the kind of man my father was!" or "I'll give my kids a much better homelife than my mother gave me," but who end up being exactly like the parent they're trying not to mirror. When we think about something, even as a negative example, our thoughts draw us toward it. This is why Scripture encourages us to set our minds on things of God and to think about "such things" as godly character traits,[5] while staying away from the negative attributes of our past. Following the list of negative character traits and behaviors at the end of Romans 1, for instance, the apostle Paul doesn't tell them to strive not to be like that anymore; he informs them that they *aren't* that anymore. Don't push back against them; respond to the pull of godliness. In the article "Pastor, Why Do You Want a Big Church?" on The Gospel Coalition blog, Graham Heslop suggests, "Perhaps we do need to explore pastors' hidden motivations behind the desire for a big church after all." He offered the balanced approach that "the desire for large thriving ministries is surely in many cases a healthy and prayerful longing for evangelism and conversions. However, we are deceiving ourselves if we deny that mixed motives may lie beneath."[6]

We tell ourselves that our desire for bigger is motivated by Christ and His kingdom, and the needs of our congregation and community, but we know better. Or we should. We're not running at an unsustainable pace for *them*, we're doing it for *ourselves*. We've bought into the lie that the church can't move forward unless we *make* it go there. We tell ourselves we're building bigger churches to serve the kingdom, but a lot of it is building bigger barns to feed our own egos. We need to let it go. We're the only ones who want this. Christ is not a drill sergeant, demanding that we do more, preach better, lead more innovatively, streamline the church's systems, or get bigger each year—neither are most church members. That's on us. What if we decided to stop the cycle, slow down, and put some pastoring into our pastoring? Would our families be upset? Likely the opposite. Would the congregation push back? They'd likely feel relieved. Would we disappoint Jesus? Hardly. If we slowed down enough, we might discover that the Savior we've been working so hard for is waiting for us to do that, so He can take the wheel again and lead His church—and us—like He promised He would.

If you feel trapped by the endless obsession of chasing bigness, there's some very good news. The key to freedom is not a mystery; it's already in your hand. We can reverse this if we're willing to acknowledge and address the problem. But first we must take a clear, unflinching look at how we got here. Getting bigger is such an assumed part of our church leadership conversations that most of us aren't aware that numerical growth wasn't a central concern for most of church history. And it wasn't so long ago that it all changed.

Part 2

FORGOTTEN BUT NOT GONE: THE SCIENCE AND HISTORY OF CHURCH GROWTH

Chapter 3

Original Intent: Donald McGavran's Big Idea

*"Will your church grow?" These are actually
the wrong questions to ask. Jesus never used
these things as metrics of success.*

Francis Chan

Every great idea has unintended consequences. The Church
Growth Movement (CGM) is no exception. And, yes, the
Church Growth Movement was a great idea. As conceived, designed,
and implemented by its founder, Donald McGavran, it was a world-
changer. But McGavran was not naïve. Unlike most pioneers and
innovators, he was acutely aware of the potential downsides of his
ideas. In fact, he identified them and structured his nascent movement to avoid them for as long as he could, until the inevitable took
place. And when it did, everything McGavran feared would happen
did happen, just as he had predicted.

So, who was Donald McGavran? How did he come up with
the idea he called Church Growth? What problems did he antici-
pate and try to avoid? What went wrong? And why did this one
man's ideas catch on so overwhelmingly that they became the way

an entire generation practiced pastoral ministry? And, maybe most importantly, what comes next?

Here is the beginning of that story and of the answers to those questions.

The McGavran Factor

Church growth has burrowed so deeply into our psyches that most pastors haven't considered that these ideas had to come from somewhere. I imagine if you asked one hundred pastors, "Who is the most influential thinker and writer in the history of church growth?" you would likely get dozens of answers, and I doubt if even the most well-known names would get more than thirty votes. But according to Nelson Searcy of Church Leader Insights, there's only one possible answer. "Donald McGavran is the single most influential thinker on how we do ministry today. His life's work is the foundation of what you and I know about growing healthy, impactful churches. . . . I would be surprised if you're aware of the full impact his work has had on today's church—and, more specifically, on you."[1] That bold assertion comes in the first paragraph of Nelson Searcy's foreword to Gary L. McIntosh's definitive book, *Donald A. McGavran: A Biography of the Twentieth Century's Premiere Missiologist*. But by the end of his book, McIntosh makes the case that Searcy's statement deserves to be taken very seriously. I have come to agree with Searcy and McIntosh that we cannot fully understand where we are and how we think about church leadership today without knowing the basics of McGavran's work. His impact is that large—and certainly worth exploring.

Donald A. McGavran and his wife, Mary, served as missionaries in India from 1923 to 1954, where he became fascinated with reports of breakout movements in which people were coming to Jesus *en masse*, sometimes as entire villages. At first, notes Elmer Towns, one of McGavran's early students, McGavran was "skeptical about whether these claims were biblical," referring to them as "half-baked missions work," but he eventually came to believe that "God was blessing that way of growth."[2]

Through his research, McGavran developed four questions that became the foundation of the Church Growth Movement:

1. What are the *causes* of church growth?
2. What are the *barriers* to church growth?
3. What are the factors that can make the Christian faith a *movement* among some populations?
4. What *principles* of church growth are reproducible?[3]

Questions 1, 2, and 4 have become so commonplace in church leadership that it's hard to imagine that they weren't even a part of the conversation until McGavran outlined them in the late 1960s, and that they weren't mainstreamed until the 1980s.

Near the end of his time in India, McGavran finished the manuscript for his first book, originally titled *How Peoples Become Christian*. Before publishing it, he visited Africa to study similar types of Christian people movements. After arriving back in the US, he went to Yale University under a research fellowship to update his book, now titled *The Bridges of God*. Since its publication in 1955, it has been recognized as the first book about church growth,[4] being hailed as "the Magna Carta of the Church Growth Movement"[5] and the "birth certificate"[6] of church growth.

After serving in various mission fields from 1953–1961, McGavran moved to Eugene, Oregon, in 1960, where he launched the Institute of Church Growth.[7] Over the next few years, McGavran and his compatriots* wrote a stack of books and articles that, while

*These included Alan Tippett, John Huegel, Jack Taylor, James Sunda, Roy Shearer, and others.

virtually forgotten now, strengthened their commitment to this research and built the foundation for what would become the science and industry of Church Growth.[8]

Fuller and the Church Growth Institute

Donald McGavran had one of the all-time great third acts in ministry. Based on his groundbreaking writing and teaching, he was invited to become the founding dean of the School of World Mission and Church Growth Institute (SWM-CGI) at Fuller Theological Seminary in 1965, at sixty-eight years of age. The school started modestly, with the original student body limited to "fifty career missionaries taught by a full-time faculty of six, along with several visiting lecturers."[9] But Thom Rainer has called this connection between McGavran and Fuller "perhaps the most important development in holding the Church Growth Movement together."

One of McGavran's early students was C. Peter Wagner, who had not been a fan of *The Bridges of God*, originally referring to it as "cockroach food."[10] When he discovered that the author of this "food" was teaching at his alma mater, he returned to see what all the fuss was about. He quickly became convinced of the efficacy of McGavran's approach and would soon become its most ardent and well-known supporter and promoter, eventually being acknowledged as McGavran's "successor both in style and interests."[11]

In 1970, McGavran wrote his second landmark book, *Understanding Church Growth*, which outlined the science of Church Growth. By this time, church growth (the idea) and Church Growth (the movement) were receiving a lot of attention, while his critics were finding and flexing their voices. Among the most frequent criticisms were that numbers were all that mattered to McGavran. Any honest reading of his actual words would show that this was simply not true. The foundational truths of biblical Christianity, especially the atonement of Jesus and the centrality of the cross in evangelism, were irreducible elements in every step of his philosophy of ministry. He may have been one of the world's most ambitious innovators when it came to methodology, but his approach to theology was solidly conservative and evangelical. As Rick Warren acknowledged, McGavran "brilliantly challenged the conventional wisdom of his day about what made churches grow," while holding firmly to "a biblical basis and simple but passionate logic."[12]

Now we come to the part of his story that shocked me. Not only did McGavran not pursue the growing of larger churches like most of his American counterparts, he actively resisted allowing ministers from North America to attend SWM-CGI. For instance, he only accepted students who were mid-career missionaries and who met three qualifications:

1. Field experience
2. Fluency in a language other than English
3. Wide knowledge of one's field, mission, and its indigenous churches[13]

This intentionally excluded almost every US-based pastor. As Gary McIntosh told me when we appeared together on a podcast, McGavran didn't trust what American pastors would do with his principles:

> The original intent of the Church Growth Movement was to help churches of all sizes, but particularly small churches, to be more effective and fruitful in making disciples [but] somewhere along the line . . . the church growth movement got co-opted, I think, or another word might be hijacked, by kind of the more popular church growth opinions that were driven by the megachurches.[14]

This is what McGavran had feared would happen. In the early church growth books and pamphlets by McGavran and his team, "there's no intended desire to create megachurches, *per se*, it's to help churches be more creative in making disciples."[15]

We've seen already that the first students of CGI were mid-career missionaries with non-US field experience. In part, this was because McGavran saw Church Growth primarily as a foreign missions endeavor, but it was also because he was paying attention to the big-church ideas of American pastors like Robert Schuller, Jack Hyles, D. James Kennedy, Rex Humbard, and W. A. Criswell. These churches were being used as examples of how to grow ministries to enormous sizes, but this American-grown approach was very different from McGavran's focus. While we often see those pastors and McGavran through a single church growth lens, there's no evidence that any of them had studied McGavran's research. Most of them couldn't have, since the growth of their churches preceded the publication of most of the SWM-CGI resources.

On the surface, their church growth ideas might have looked similar, and church leaders in subsequent generations have built principles from all of them, but the popular pastors of that era came from very different starting points than McGavran and the SWM-CGI team.[16] These popular pastors were sharing how growth happened in *their* church, while McGavran and SWM-CGI were promoting transferable principles from *wherever* the gospel was thriving and churches were growing.[17] This principle of transferability is one of the keys that makes McGavran's research stand out from the pack, and why he is considered the father of Church Growth. The next generation of Church Growth proponents would adopt what missiologist Harvie M. Conn called McGavran's "refined specialized vocabulary"[18] of church growth language, but most followed the principles of the other church growth stream. (More on that in chapter 4.)

One question that is often asked about McGavran's work is,

For someone who supported evangelism so strongly, why did he call his ideas Church Growth? "He coined the term church growth as a way to describe the essential work of the Great Commission," wrote Nelson Searcy. "At its core, church growth is about effective evangelism; it's about a passionate focus on reaching people for Jesus. Nothing more, nothing less."[19]

In 1972, McGavran finally relented to the constant pressure from US pastors and from some within SWM-CGI, agreeing to teach a class with C. Peter Wagner for North American church leaders. This class is considered the spark for the flame that became the American Church Growth Movement.

Now we can see that while our church growth conversation came into stark visibility in the last two generations, it didn't spring from nowhere. This neither justifies our subsequent numerical obsession nor blames McGavran, but it's helpful to know that it has a history. But this is not church growth's only origin story. While McGavran's principles were catching on and growing from a trickle into a river, another river had already been flowing for generations. As it turns out, there wasn't just one Church Growth Movement, there were two. Now that we've seen the McGavran stream, we'll look at the other stream, one that actually preceded McGavran by a lot. Church growth, welcome to the United States of America.

Chapter 4

(Pre)Made in America

*The typical assumption of most books on church
and ministry—even those written more recently
in the missional church field—is the idea that
the church's job is to grow. A healthy church is a
church that grows bigger. My argument is
that this assumption is built not on the gospel
but on the American narrative.*

Tim Suttle

The Church Growth Movement feels uniquely American.
The number-crunching entrepreneurial spirit of CGM feels like
it has *Made in America* grandly emblazoned across its face in red,
white, and blue neon. But as we've seen, though the founder of CGM
was American, as was the school where the movement developed
into a systemic approach, it had been birthed in India and nursed
in Africa. Donald McGavran was not CGM's father/planter, but its
midwife/discoverer. He didn't create it as much as he noticed it, assessed it, and presented it to the world. McGavran was an astute
observer of culture. He knew if he started teaching his church growth
theories in his home country that they would be changed, adapted,
and used in ways he never intended.

So why does CGM and the obsession to grow bigger churches

feel so distinctly American? That also involves some fascinating history. From the Puritan desire for freedom, to the inconceivable size of the continent they explored, to the country's founding documents, its economic realities, its battles with racism, its blend of the holy with the profane, its political structure, and more, the United States is uniquely suited to be the place where McGavran's movement would take hold, then morph into something he both foresaw and dreaded.

Certainly, there are megachurches outside the United States. Africa, for instance, is home to several of the biggest congregations on earth. But even they trace their roots back to American soil. In *Megachurch Christianity Reconsidered*, Dr. Wanjiru M. Gitau wrote about the massive Mavuno church in Nairobi, Kenya, where she spent several years on staff before becoming a research fellow of the Center for Religion and Civic Culture at the University of Southern California. With help from research conducted by historian Mark Shaw, she posits that "nearly all such revival movements, even the African indigenous ones, retrace their roots to eighteenth-century evangelical Christianity through the missionary movement,"[1] including its "accompanying pragmatism."[2]

To get a grasp on this stream of church growth thought, let's take another tour, this time through American history, adding the elements of geography, religion, government, and economics as we go. The confluence of these ingredients in the United States had a massive effect on how we worship and perceive the role of the church today. If you come from another nation, stick with me. This affects you too.

America, the Big

From the late 1400s through the early 1900s, while the rest of the world shuffled into middle or old age, the Americas were sprinting into adolescence. The earliest European arrivals sailed the deadly waters of the North Atlantic to put as much distance as possible between themselves and corrupt power structures (governmental and ecclesiastical). These structures had controlled every aspect of their lives in Europe, especially their freedom to worship as they chose and to keep what money they earned for themselves and their family. The new arrivals struggled to come to grips with a land that was bigger, wealthier, harsher, more promising, and more populated than anyone had expected. The original settlers came for religious and economic freedom, and the combination of those two qualities blended on these new shores in a way that had never happened anywhere before. Certainly, faith and finance have always done an uneasy dance together, with everyone from popes and kings to hermits and prophets either pursuing or denouncing mammon with great vigor, often at the same time. But it was in America where these two essential human elements seemed like they might find a state of equilibrium like nowhere else.

That hope received an enormous setback in 1619 when privateers ("a pirate with papers")[3] aboard the White Lion sailed into Point Comfort, Virginia, near Jamestown.[4] This was the first time on record that humans were brought to North America to be exchanged for money, goods, or services.[5] In the ensuing years, economic pressures won out over Christian (and simply humane) virtues when slavery became a fact of life for the agriculturally rich southern states. In the years before mechanization, the planting and harvesting of crops like cotton and tobacco were so backbreakingly labor intensive that those of primarily white European ancestry embraced the enslavement of their fellow human beings as a way not just to survive financially, but (for a few) to become outrageously wealthy.

While secular historians emphasize the financial and racial roots of American history, Christian historians tend to focus on the nation's religious roots. For any accurate, honest appraisal, both deserve consideration. This battle is fought nowhere more vehemently than in how each group approaches the most important document in American history (and arguably the most important of the last three-hundred-plus years), the US Constitution and Bill of Rights. This brilliant and groundbreaking document was a product of the economic and religious realities of its time. It is filled with elevating, noble phrases as in the First Amendment, which states "Congress shall make no law respecting an establishment of religion, or prohibiting the free exercise thereof; or abridging the freedom of speech, or of the press; or the right of the people peaceably to assemble, and to petition the Government for a redress of grievances."[6] But the Constitution also contains horrific compromises on their values such as the clause that states that enslaved people would only count as three-fifths of a person when calculating the population for taxation and representation.*

From their first arrival, Europeans tried to fathom the size of this new (to them) land. For hundreds of years, the expansion was slow. Then in 1804, Thomas Jefferson commissioned army captain Meriwether Lewis to head up an exploratory team to discover the Northwest Passage—a term commonly used for what they believed would be a river-based route to the West Coast. In *Canoeing the Mountains*, Tod Bolsinger (with help from Dayton Duncan and Ken Burns) relates a momentous day when Lewis and his coleader William Clark reached the Lemhi Pass on the Continental Divide. They expected to see the west half of the continent laid out in front of them more or less like the eastern half was—challenging landscape, but sloping toward the Pacific Ocean. Instead, they beheld the Rocky Mountains. As they tried to comprehend the breathtaking beauty, they realized that "the dream of an easy water route across the continent—a dream stretching back to Christopher Columbus—was shattered."[7] The land they were determined to conquer—indeed that they believed, in their

---

*The precise wording of the three-fifths clause is, "Representatives and direct Taxes shall be apportioned among the several States which may be included within this Union, according to their respective Numbers, which shall be determined by adding to the whole Number of free Persons, including those bound to Service for a Term of Years, and excluding Indians not taxed, three fifths of all other Persons." From the US Constitution, Article I, Section 2.

hubris, they were destined by God to conquer—would put up far more resistance than anyone could have imagined.

Humans think we shape the land. And in many ways, for good and for ill, we do. But we often forget how the land shapes us. In North America, the size, abundance, and virtual impenetrability of the land shaped the way we saw ourselves, the way we treated others, and the way we considered our relationship with God in far deeper, longer-lasting ways than most of us have a clue about or would like to admit. The vastness of the West created a new breed of colorful characters, including the pioneers, cowboys, entrepreneurs, con artists, railroad barons, and revivalists of the aptly named Wild West.

As America expanded, it experienced three great revivals: the Great Awakening, the (not very creatively named) Second Great Awakening, and the Third Great Awakening. The Great Awakening took place from the 1730s–1770s under the leadership of preachers like Jonathan Edwards, George Whitefield, and John and Charles Wesley. In this new land there was no state religion, so preachers, churches, and revivalists were free to interpret Scripture on their own. They could preach to whomever would listen, while building churches that fit their own theological leanings. This was the start of the religion/entrepreneurialism hybrid that continues to thrive today. As author Susan Cain notes:

> Even the Christianity of early American religious revivals, dating back to the First Great Awakening of the eighteenth century, depended on the showmanship of ministers who were considered successful if they caused crowds of normally reserved people to weep and shout and generally lose their decorum. "Nothing gives me more pain and distress than to see a minister standing almost motionless, coldly plodding on as a mathematician would calculate the distance of the Moon from the Earth," complained a religious newspaper in 1837.[8]

The Second Great Awakening "was even more explosive than the first," writes Frances FitzGerald in her essential book, *The Evangelicals*, "creating a simpler, more democratic faith that accorded with the spirit of the new country."[9] Spanning the 1790s to the 1840s, it was led by more controversial figures than the first, including early preachers like James McGready, John McGee, and Barton W. Stone, then becoming a little more respectable under the likes of Timothy Dwight, Lyman Beecher, Nathaniel W. Taylor, and Asahel Nettleton. In its later years, the country met its most well-known and impactful character, the evangelist Charles Grandison Finney. Starting in New York state, Finney blazed a trail across the country and into its heart like no one before him. Temperance became a byword, with entire cities going "dry" overnight. Before Finney, "early-nineteenth-century Americans drank prodigiously—perhaps four times as much as Americans do today."[10] Finney preached against slavery and for women's rights. He also promoted better education for all children, eventually leading to the public school system. He and his followers also protested the forced expulsion of Cherokees from their tribal land in 1838.[11]

The Second Great Awakening created massive growth in denominations, especially the Methodists, Presbyterians, and Baptists. It was also the beginning of the Mormons, Seventh Day Adventists, and Unitarians, among others. The latter three are evidence that there was a small but significant group of Americans who were so determined to distinguish themselves from their forebears that they were willing to create and follow new ways of believing and belonging, with minimal connections to traditional Christian beliefs. American expressions of Christianity were now visibly and fundamentally different from their European roots. This also brought another more subtle but quite significant change. According to Glenn Packiam and Melanie Ross, "While Jonathan Edwards during the First Great Awakening described 'revival' as a 'marvelous work of God,' Charles

Finney about a hundred years later argued that revival was the result of employing the 'appropriate means.' The goal was the conversion of souls through whatever means worked." As a result, "without realizing it, many of us are heirs to Finney's legacy" of pragmatic results over God's ineffable work.[12]

The Third Great Awakening (though not identified by that name by many historians) spanned the late 1850s through the early 1900s and gave birth to the Holiness movement, the Nazarene church, the Pentecostal movement, and others. Unlike the first two awakenings, this one was cross-oceanic. In England, its most well-known preachers included Londoners like William and Catherine Booth (who founded the Salvation Army) and Charles Spurgeon.

In America, its premiere names were D. L. Moody of Chicago, former baseball player Billy Sunday, healing-evangelist-turned-pastor-turned-denominational-leader Aimee Semple McPherson, and pastor/author Norman Vincent Peale. It is from these last four preachers (Moody, Sunday, McPherson, and Peale) that a direct line can be drawn to the preaching style, systems, and crowds of today's evangelicals, especially to megachurches and mass-media ministry. Dwight L. Moody (1837–1899) was an innovator who erected many of the pillars that modern evangelicalism sits on, including tent revivals, Sunday school, Bible schools, and Christian publishing.[13] He regularly spoke "to audiences of ten thousand to twenty thousand people," putting the salvation call at the apex of the meeting.[14] Billy Sunday (1862–1935) set the template for the modern barnstorming preacher, stirring the crowd with controversial, crowd pleasing, red meat sermons, most famously, "Booze, or, Get on the Water Wagon," which helped to make him "the most successful evangelist America had ever known at the time.[15] McPherson (1890–1944), popularly known as "Sister Aimee," was a master of the on-stage spectacle, regularly impressing stars like Charlie Chaplin, William Randolph Hearst, and heavyweight champion Jack Johnson. She built and pastored Angelus Temple, a massive (and still impressive) domed cathedral in the Echo Park neighborhood of Los Angeles. She also started a radio station, LIFE Bible College, and the Church of the Foursquare Gospel. Norman Vincent Peale (1898–1993) pastored Marble Collegiate Church in New York for over fifty years, but is mostly known as the author of the bestselling book *The Power of Positive Thinking*. He is widely acknowledged as the pioneer of the feel-good, success-oriented, prosperity-based Christianity that has been echoed by pastors like Robert Schuller and Joel Osteen.

> **When you have an open market, not just in finance but in religion, the size of the crowd brings an air of credibility.**

According to FitzGerald, while Christianity had developed slowly and deliberately in pre-printing-press Europe, the American Awakenings were said to be "a religion of the heart, as opposed to the head. And everywhere, they introduced a new idea of conversion as a sudden, overwhelming experience of God's grace. . . . They undermined the established churches, led to the separation of church and state, and created a marketplace of religious ideas in which new sects and denominations survived and flourished."[16] When you have an open market, not just in finance but in religion, the size of the crowd brings an air of credibility, along with the cash to keep it sustainable, and it acts as a dangerous temptation.

Along the way, these elements were combined in new, previously unknown ways, inspired by the element of American government, specifically, the First Amendment of the Bill of Rights. This extraordinary document is perhaps the strongest protection ever written for the rights of people to practice (or not practice) their religion without a state church or, ideally, any state interference. It's hard for Americans to imagine this, but in many European countries not only were the churches not taxed, they also received direct financial support through taxation. Several still do today.[17]

Another segment of the American constitution that has affected the church more than we realize is Article I, Section 10, known as the Contract Clause. It provides that no state may pass any "Law impairing the Obligation of Contracts."[18] This allows for a unique relationship between groups of citizens, such as an agreement between a church and its members, that holds great power separate from, and sometimes superseding, that held by the government over its peoples.

When the First Amendment cut churches off from governmental support, every church was in the position of having to raise their own funds. Suddenly, having a bigger church meant a greater giving base. This is where economics played a uniquely different role in America than it had in any nation previously. Since European churches were on the receiving end of state taxes, most had no need to attract huge crowds to pay their bills. In America, every church, pastor, evangelist, and denomination had the freedom to believe and say what they wanted, and churches could make binding agreements among its members, but now they also had to raise their own funds.

Without a state church, or the taxes collected for it, and aided by the Contract Clause and the First Amendment, the entrepreneurial and competitive approach to church came into being. As a result, according to Nathan O. Hatch in *The Democratization of American Christianity*, "competition in the religious marketplace muted the appeal of orthodox churches and amplified the message of insurgents."[19] This fed into the myth of American meritocracy.

The Rise of Meritocracy

From its founding, Americans have argued over whether we are supposed to be a republic or a direct democracy. Thus, the names of the two main political parties, Republicans and Democrats. But many of those arguments are built on a premise that both sides agree on—that we should be a meritocracy. If a democracy is rule by the people, and republicanism is rule by the people's representatives (also known as a "democratic republic" or "indirect democracy"), then meritocracy is rule by those who have earned it by their merit. It's the presumption that *our side* deserves to rule because we've shown the competence to do so ("Our candidate delivered on his promises"), while the other side is framed as incompetent ("They failed to deliver") and doesn't merit the right to rule.

You don't need to read very far into current church leadership literature to see how meritocracy has taken root. Books, blogs, conferences, and podcasts that champion a business like approach to church meritocracy attract far more readers, listeners, and attenders than those that emphasize being a simple pastoral presence. One exception to that rule is Eugene Peterson, who addressed this issue many times. As one of the most widely read and respected pastors of his generation, he became very skeptical about the meritocratic approach to pastoral ministry.

His biographer, Winn Collier, recounted an episode in which Peterson's pastoral supervisor "handed Eugene an overstuffed red three-ring binder filled with instructions on everything one could possibly think of related to forming a new church."[20]

> Whatever problem Eugene might face as a pastor, he need only run his finger down the index and find appropriate instructions. . . . But Eugene noticed how little God had to do with any of it. He sensed something elemental had shifted—from God, the Cross, the Resurrection, and the living Spirit, to finding out what people wanted. And then giving it to them. Petersen explained, "The ink on my ordination papers wasn't even dry before I was being told by experts, so-called,

in the field of church that my main task was to run a church
after the manner of my brother and sister Christians who
run service stations, grocery stores, corporations, banks, hos-
pitals, and financial services."[21]

This is the unintended, but unavoidable result of obsessing over
numerical growth at the cost of everything else. The American landscape has simply given that obsession a new look and feel. And it
happened so quickly and with so much else to divert our attention
that we haven't taken the time to slow down, step back, and properly
assess what it's doing to us, our churches, and our witness to the
world. Scot McKnight and Laura Barringer address this issue in *A
Church Called Tov*. "Something radical has seeped into the church in
the last fifty years. The American meritocracy has reshaped pastors
and churches, and a new culture has taken root, based on achieve-
ment and accomplishment rather than holiness and Christlikeness."[22]
There's a lot about meritocracy that is good and healthy. Receiving
a promotion at work because you're better at your job, rather than
because you share the last name of the boss, is good. But meritocracy
has its downsides, especially in the church, where everything we receive from God is based not on merit but on grace, and everything we
do for each other is supposed to be based on grace as well.

In such a climate, the role of the pastor has become completely
redefined in many quarters, based far more on the business and meritocracy model than on Scripture. McKnight and Barringer write:

> Churches today have been so greatly influenced by meritoc-
> racy, by the achievement and accomplishment culture of the
> business world, that they now define *pastor* with business-
> culture terms instead of biblical terms. In business terms, a
> pastor is a "leader," and *leader* is defined by the meritocratic
> system of American culture. But when pastors are defined

primarily as *leaders*—or *entrepreneurs* or *visionaries*—they've already ceased to be pastors in any biblical sense.[23]

Take a tour through the most popular pastoral and church growth materials and you'll see that this is not an exaggeration. The entire process emphasizes performance over character. And that's what we get.

While there is much evidence that the Great Awakenings were indeed a revival of the heart and spirit for hundreds of thousands, maybe millions of people, there were also many abuses of power and a great deal of emotional manipulation. You get far more money from people by courting controversy and fighting enemies (real or imagined) than you do by staying with the slow, unspectacular work of hands-on pastoral care. This trend continues today in anger blogs, conspiracy theory videos, Twitter feuds, Facebook memes, and whatever new form of electronic communication has become popular by the time you read this. Those who chase clicks and likes in the twenty-first century are the electronic children of those who printed pamphlets to chase money and power in the eighteenth and nineteenth centuries.

When these elements of America's relatively young history, entrepreneurial approach to economics, unspeakably vast geography, freedom of religion, people-led government, and meritocracy came together, they gave the world something it had never seen before, and that every nation, government, and people have been affected by ever since: the entrepreneurial church. According to Skye Jethani, "Ministry in the United States is modeled primarily on capitalism, with pastors functioning as a church's sales force, and evangelism as its marketing strategy. . . . The First Amendment prohibited state sanctioned religion. Therefore, faith, like the buying of material goods, became a matter of personal choice."[24]

Of course, the church that Jesus came to establish was here long before the Americas were even dreamed of, and it will exist in eternity long after America and all the other world systems have ceased to be. But we'd be foolish not to take a serious look at how this nation that George Washington called the "great experiment"[25] has affected every area of life and has impacted every part of the world in ways both positive and negative.

Chapter 5

The Streams Combine

Religion brought forth riches, and the daughter
devoured the mother.

Francis Bacon

In the summer between my third and fourth years of Bible college in Santa Cruz, California, I interned at a church in Toronto, Canada. When I arrived, the pastor handed me a book. It was *Your Church Has Real Possibilities* by Robert Schuller. I was told to read it cover to cover as quickly as possible because, "This explains how we do everything here." I walked out of his office a little disappointed (had I really driven all the way from California to Canada to learn from a book written by a pastor *in California*?), but also intrigued.

This was my introduction to church growth, and until quite recently, I thought it had been my introduction to the Church Growth Movement. But it wasn't CGM at all. What I didn't know was that I was being introduced to one stream of church growth—the "American stream." Over the following decades I dipped almost exclusively from that stream as I grew in my understanding of pastoral ministry. Sure, I heard about the teachings of Donald McGavran and CGM along the way, but they were marginal to me. I thought McGavran's CGM principles were just one of the boats in the church growth stream.

The pastor who gave me Schuller's book was doing what so many pastors did. He saw what the most popular, fastest growing churches were doing, then used what Gary L. McIntosh calls their *How I Did It* books to teach willing and eager students and church members.[1] While there's always something to gain by watching the examples set by others, this approach is limited in its transferability (and is often not transferable at all), adding to the great confusion and frustration of church leaders who can't duplicate what their heroes have done.

What happened to me was what happened to most young pastors-in-training in that era. We were introduced to the American stream of church growth at about the time the McGavran stream was just getting underway. Perhaps the most vivid and influential example of this is Rick Warren. Starting on the first page of the first chapter of *The Purpose Driven Church* (easily the most widely read church growth book of all time, with over one million copies sold),[2] Warren describes how he was following the example of W. A. Criswell (a major figure in the American stream) when he found an article about Donald McGavran that "dramatically impacted the direction of my life as much as my encounter with Criswell had."[3] While a personal meeting with Criswell had given Warren the inspiration to grow a big church, it was the writings of McGavran that added the church growth language, along with the desire "to invest the rest of my life discovering the principles—biblical, cultural, and leadership principles—that produce healthy, growing churches."[4]

Like Rick Warren, so many pastors of that era adopted the terminology of McGavran and the Church Growth Movement while they were swimming not in McGavran's *how to do it* stream, but in the American *how I did it* stream—but unlike Warren, most of us didn't know it. And that confusion is just as prevalent today as it was in the 1980s. Maybe more so.

Let's extend the metaphor.

The great manufacturing city of Pittsburgh was built where the

Allegheny and Monongahela rivers meet. Upstream, the rivers flow from separate sources under different names, but after Pittsburgh, they have a single, new name—the Ohio River. Then, even farther downstream, the Ohio joins the Mississippi and loses its name to that great river. Most of what we see in mainstream church leadership today is like that except, instead of the smaller rivers taking on the name of the biggest river, when the McGavran stream flowed into the American stream we used McGavran's term, "church growth," for all of it. But it was almost entirely American.

Donald McGavran had anticipated this, which is why he resisted the merger as long as he could. And perhaps, if he hadn't been near retirement (his early seventies) when Church Growth came in like a flood, he might have had the time and strength to resist it longer and have an even greater impact. But, as with the mighty Mississippi, some movements are almost impossible to resist. It's not that the McGavran stream didn't change things. It certainly did. From the term church growth, to his now obvious "four church leadership questions" about *causes, barriers, movements,* and *principles,* we're all swimming in the water of the McGavran stream. But the American stream is the Mississippi: large, overwhelming, and seemingly unstoppable.

If you're reading the popular church leaders, you're primarily learning from the American stream. And you're being affected by it in ways you don't recognize. This is true even if you live and minister outside the United States. The only way to understand the differences between the streams and try to reclaim a new way forward is to go upstream and use the history we learned in these last chapters to understand what the streams looked like before they were irrevocably joined. Then maybe we can forge a new way forward.

The Streams, Summarized

Here are several of the key lessons we can extract from our upstream journey we've just taken:

First, church growth in the American stream tends to be filled with *how I did it* examples from the pastors of the largest and fastest growing churches. My experience with Robert Schuller's book is an example of this. In contrast, the McGavran stream was based on discovering and understanding *how to do it*.

Second, the American stream is a "how this works" approach. It's less about asking questions and more about providing answers based on specific examples. On the other hand, McGavran starts, not with answers, but with one big question; "How *does* this work?"

Third, the American stream was based on the dynamic personalities and skills of numerically successful pastors and Christian leaders, while the McGavran stream was based on research methods.

Fourth, in the American stream, "success" is measured almost exclusively by attendance. Not only do we tend to learn from the biggest, fastest growing churches, but it's not uncommon for the pastors of those churches to refuse to believe they could learn or come under the ecclesiastical authority of pastors from smaller churches, as we saw in Mark Driscoll's example. At first, the McGavran stream may seem like it's doing the same—measuring success by numbers. The difference, however, is that McGavran didn't emphasize church attendance; he was laser focused on genuine, verifiable conversion experiences. He even coined the now-common term "transfer growth" to describe this phenomenon, which he said "is not growth at all in terms of net additions to the body of Christ."[5]

Fifth, the American stream has a very *individualistic* approach to leadership, growth, and salvation. We follow *individual* pastors hoping to see growth in *individual* congregations through *individualized* salvation and discipleship experiences. In contrast, the McGavran stream was built on the idea of studying people-movements. McGavran witnessed entire families, towns, and clans coming to salvation and he wanted to understand how and why this was happening.

Sixth, the American stream started by looking to individual, numerically growing congregations. After attempting to discover the principles that made them work, they tried to replicate similar results in other, more diverse places. Donald McGavran went the other way, starting with a wide-ranging study of what God was doing in places as diverse as India, Africa, and the United States. He boiled those ideas down to universal principles, which could be used in individual congregations, contextualized for specific situations.

Seventh, and perhaps most controversial, are the two very different approaches they take to the *homogenous unit principle* (sometimes called the *homogenous church principle*). I was introduced to this phrase within the American stream. What I was taught was that a church will grow faster if you choose a specific type of individual to target, then aim all your resources at reaching that demographic. If you narrow your mission field to one people-group, you'll overcome one perceived obstacle to faith—that some people experience discomfort worshiping with different races, ethnicities, economic standings, and so on.

When I heard this idea, I rejected it wholeheartedly. I still do. And since this definition of the homogenous unit principle was presented to me as one of the primary teachings of Donald McGavran, I rejected him and his teachings as well. In my more recent research I discovered that, while Donald McGavran did in fact coin the term homogeneous church principle, what he meant by it was the opposite of what I had been taught. During his decades in India, McGavran noticed that when someone came to Christ, they had to deal with a serious issue that we have no understanding of in America: caste.

Caste is still a huge part of Indian life and culture, especially in smaller cities and towns. It involves a mix of ethnicity, geography, vocation, culture, and economics that I can't even begin to comprehend from my Western perspective. But I do know this: your caste is a core aspect of your identity, and it's virtually unchangeable. The caste you're born into is the caste you'll live and die in. Having relationships or conversations across caste lines is fraught with perilous complications. Caste is so ingrained in Indian culture that if a person hears about salvation through Jesus from someone of a different caste (or a different country, like America or England), they expect that becoming a Christian means crossing caste lines and turning their back on their family and culture. One essential premise of McGavran's homogenous unit principle was that when we help people within one caste reach out to others within their own caste, they don't start with the faulty thinking that coming to Christ means changing castes or rejecting the positive aspects of their culture.

The homogenous unit principle, as presented to me in an American context, felt divisive and racist. But as presented originally by McGavran from an Indian context, it was and is unifying and anti-racist. While the American stream presented the homogenous unit principle to me as a way of walling people off from one another, McGavran's original premise was to build bridges between people, thus the title of his book, *The Bridges of God.*

Finally, the American stream celebrates the entrepreneurial pastor. We have elevated the entrepreneurial pastor to near mythic levels, sometimes at the cost of downplaying, even insulting, the humble, caregiving pastor. This may be where the American and McGavran streams seem the most similar. As you'll recall, this was one of the places where McGavran received serious pushback when he proposed basing missionary budgets on results, not just on previous allocations. The differences may be subtle, but they're significant. McGavran's idea was not to target funds based on the entrepreneurial skill of the presenter, but on the potential receptivity of the harvest field. In the American stream, instead of targeting our attention and resources where people are coming to Christ, we tend to emulate big, fast-growing churches with little or no consideration for the fact that most aren't operating in ripe harvest fields, but in populous, growing communities where Christians are moving in large numbers.

As seen in the following side-by-side table, these two streams were destined to cause great conflict when they flowed together. This is why McGavran worked for as long as he could to keep them separated.

AMERICAN STREAM VS. MCGAVRAN STREAM

American Stream	McGavran Stream
How I Did It	How to Do It
How This Works	How Does This Work?
Personality-Based	Research-Based
Attendance-Driven	Conversion-Driven
Individualistic	People Movements
Homogenous Unit Builds Walls	Homogenous Unit Builds Bridges
Entrepreneur-Targeted Resources	Harvest-Targeted Resources

No wonder the average pastor is leading from a place of confusion and frustration that seems to grow rather than diminish the more we read and listen to numerically successful church leaders. We're drinking from a river that has been formed from two very different, and often contradictory, streams, and almost no one is aware of it. Once they merged, they created a conflict of ideas in which the smaller, newer trickle (McGavran's) would inevitably be overwhelmed by the much older and massively larger torrent (American).

There were three primary results following the combining of the American and McGavran streams:

1. The relentless race for "bigger" continued unabated. That river was too big and too numerically successful to be contained.

2. The language and some of the methods of the McGavran stream provided cover for the relentless obsession with bigness from the American stream. This appears to be some of what concerned McGavran about Americans adopting his ideas—that we'd co-opt the language without adopting the methodology.

3. This happened virtually invisibly. When you live downriver, it's impossible to know what happened upriver until someone goes there and reports on where our current situation derived from.

Now, let's turn to two elements of American life that have contributed greatly to our size obsession in more recent years: suburbs and technology. Neither of these are exclusive to the United States, but both are woven into the fabric and identity of life in America in ways that are different and more ingrained than anywhere else. And especially in the lives of my generation, the Baby Boomers.

Chapter 6

Boom: The Impact of Suburbs on the Church

*When the twentieth century arrived, a perfect
storm of big business, urbanization, and mass
immigration blew the population into the cities.
… Americans responded to these pressures by
trying to become salesmen who could sell not only
their company's latest gizmo but also themselves.*

SUSAN CAIN

M egachurches are not unheard of, historically. The authors of
High on God: How Megachurches Won the Heart of America note
that "megachurches have always been a part of the Christian tradition, from the early cathedrals of the Catholic tradition to the great
Eastern Orthodox basilica of Constantinople."[1] In America, Charles
Finney's Broadway Tabernacle (seating 2,400, with room for 4,000),[2]
Moody Church (seating 4,040),[3] and Aimee Semple McPherson's
Angelus Temple (seating 5,300)[4] have been around since 1836, 1864,
and 1923, respectively. But churches of such size have been so rare
that there wasn't even a term for them until "megachurch" showed
up in print in 1978.[5] But once they arrived, they came to stay. And
to multiply.

In the United States, "the rapid proliferation of these churches since the 1970s, and especially in the past few decades, is a distinctive social phenomenon," wrote Scott Thumma and David Travis in *Beyond Megachurch Myths*. "In 1969, Elmer Towns . . . listed sixteen churches with two thousand or more attendees weekly." By 1984 there were seventy, in 1990 the number was 310. By 2000, Thumma and Travis could verify six hundred megachurches. "From 1980 onward," they wrote, "the number of megachurches per million of population doubles every ten years."[6] That pace has slowed only slightly since 2000. In 2020, the latest year available for this book, the official number stands at 1,750, according to Aaron Earls of LifeWay Research.[7]

While the first megachurches were mostly in city centers, it's no coincidence that the rise of the megachurch didn't happen until the rise of the suburbs. "In the late 1980s, the location pattern of megachurches shifted dramatically," write Scott Thumma and David Travis. "Over 75 percent of them were now located in suburban Sunbelt states [and] the newest megachurches are predominantly locating in distant suburbs or exurbs."[8] To find out why, let's take a short but fascinating detour into the rise of the suburbs.

The Rise of the Suburbs

Until the late nineteenth century, America was mostly an agrarian society. As a result of the industrialization of cities, the Great Migration (approx. 1910–1970) saw over six million poor agricultural laborers, primarily African Americans, move from southern rural regions to northern cities, looking for work and a greater sense of personal autonomy.[9] This, along with continued European migration, swelled the cities, jamming more and more people into smaller, poorer spaces, while the ability to provide an infrastructure of water, sewage, and other essentials lagged far behind. Something had to give. What eventually "gave" was the rise of the suburbs.

When city planners build roads and houses, they use a principle called Marchetti's Constant, named after Cesare Marchetti, an Italian physicist (born 1927) who proposed that people will only commute, on average, about half an hour in each direction.[10] In *A Brief History of Motion*, Tom Standage points out that the first time we had anything that could be referred to as suburbs was at the end of horsecar lines in the 1850s. Before then, horses pulled buses along gravel or dirt paths at a top speed of about 4 mph. With the addition of railcars (the precursors to the railroads), horses could now pull commuters at 6 mph and far more comfortably. As a result, the average half-hour commute increased from two to three miles, increasing the practical size of cities by a full mile in every direction.[11] This principle has proven to be surprisingly consistent, with cities and suburbs expanding in direct correlation to our ability to get to and from work in an average of one hour return trip per day.

This slow expansion of cities continued in small increments until two big moments changed everything over a ten-year period (1947–1956). The first was the building of Levittown on Long Island, New York from 1947 to 1951. Levittown is considered the world's first planned suburban community. This new housing phenomenon allowed people to live outside the crowded, decaying city by traveling from home to work in their cars on the newly completed New York state parkway system.[12] Then in 1956, the second big moment happened. Dwight D. Eisenhower took parkways nationwide when he signed the Federal-Aid Highway Act, creating the Interstate system, enabling travel across the country on highways that went around, rather than through, cities at new levels of speed and safety.

This generated new opportunities for people to live in ways that were neither urban nor rural. With an abundance of inexpensive land, the suburbs ushered in "the golden age of the supermarket"[13] where, instead of daily visits to the mom-and-pop store around the corner, a burgeoning middle- and upper-income population loaded up the station wagon once or twice a week with goods that were larger and cheaper, while the service was faster but less personal. Former city kids no longer elbowed for play space in tiny neighborhood parks but had access to sprawling suburban greenbelts with baseball diamonds and football fields.

Churches followed, as they should. Pastors saw the burgeoning populations of people, noted the abundance of relatively inexpensive land, and moved with the crowds to the suburbs. Soon, church buildings started looking more like the malls that suburban families were getting comfortable with than the inner-city cathedrals or little white chapels of previous generations.

This is how society tends to progress. First, form follows function. We need more space, so we figure out a way to either create it or go somewhere that has it. Then, that extra space determines the next level of function. The suburbs were more than just a new *place* to live; they created a new *way* to live, along with new challenges that we're only beginning to come to terms with today. For example, the suburbs created two new forms of migration. The regional migration, followed by the daily migration. First, the regional. It's not unusual, historically, for millions of people to move in a short period of time from one region to another. What was different about the intra-regional migration to the suburbs was that it was so short (typically fewer than twenty miles, rather than hundreds of miles). Also, it caused a second migration—a daily one that had never happened before. Now, stereotypically, the father migrated to work every morning, returning home in the evening. Thus, the modern commute was born.

The Suburban Displacement

While these suburbs provided wonderful new opportunities for some, they were closed to others. Since they could only be accessed by gas-guzzling cars in most places, those in lower incomes were stuck in the cities or in dying small towns and rural areas. This also heightened the racial divide since people of color tended to be in the lower income brackets. This resulted in predominantly white suburbs, while ethnic minorities were more concentrated in inner cities. When churches followed the middle- to upper-income population into the suburbs, they typically, and not always unintentionally, abandoned racial minorities and the poor in favor of white and well-to-do populations. When middle- and upper-income people left the cities for the suburbs, they adopted not just the behaviors of the suburbs, but the ethos of the shopping mall. "Between the notion of customer is king and the expansion of highways and suburbs," wrote Wanjiru M. Gitau, "church-growth theory came as a windfall to white American Christianity."[14]

But this new double migration didn't just cause a disruption for those who were left behind. Before the suburban migration of the 1950s, migration always created a sense of displacement on geographical, emotional, and spiritual levels for those who moved away, but the permanence of the place where they arrived and the fact that they did it as a family allowed them to slowly adapt to their new environment together. Now, however, instead of living and working on a farm together or in an apartment above their family-run shop, one member of the newly displaced family was living in two locations, work and home, while the rest of the family set up house, school, stores, church, and relationships in their new home. With dad gone for nine or ten hours a day, he became physically and emotionally disconnected from the family and never fully connected to his new neighborhood.

Many of the churches that arrived in these new suburbs were modeled more after the shopping mall than the cathedral, creating a different set of expectations. If a church building looks like the mall, people subconsciously expect a consumer experience.

Recently I was at a megachurch with the architect whose company designed it. "Look around. What do you see?" he asked. "Uh, people, buildings..." I stammered. "I'll tell you what you don't see," he said. "The parking lot. Studies done for shopping malls have shown that if you can't see your car, you'll spend more time in the mall. Out of sight, out of mind." So, his firm had designed the church to create the same experience. And why not? Once you know that the lack of parking lot visibility will encourage people to hang out after church, you'd be foolish not to use that information. After all, you're not keeping them on campus to sell more products, but to help them slow down, connect with other members, and maybe sign up for a small group or ministry team.

> **Our church structures have always reflected our theological aspirations and exposed our ecclesiastical ambitions.**

Our church structures have always reflected our theological aspirations and exposed our ecclesiastical ambitions. The megachurch facility is no more or less theologically grounded than the grand cathedral or wayside chapel. The early church wouldn't have recognized any of them. But it is important that we recognize what's happening and how the changes are affecting us.

Here Come the Boomers

As suburban migration continued, it was also being amplified by a massive demographic phenomenon: the Baby Boomer generation (born 1946–1964). First, the suburbs contributed to the baby boom by giving young families much more space in which to raise larger families. Then, those growing families created the need for more suburban space.

The raw numbers are overwhelming. In 1945, the United States was an exhausted, war-weary nation of 138 million people. Over the next eighteen years, they gave birth to 76 million babies. Not only was the sheer number of births staggering, but these babies were born and came of age during everything we've looked at in this chapter. They were the first generation to benefit from the burgeoning infrastructure that included telephones, highways, cars, radios, and television. They were the kids of the families who moved first to the cities during the latter half of the Great Migration, then to the suburbs.

The parents of the Boomers had been united against a common enemy in World War II. When they came home, they wanted nothing more than a well-earned, simple, and peaceful life. But the children of this massive population increase were raised watching a series of high-impact events (the assassinations of the Kennedys and MLK, the moon landing, the Vietnam War, and the Watergate scandal) directly fed into their homes. Two decades prior, their parents had received news of the momentous events of WWII several days or weeks after they occurred through the passive media of newsprint and grainy, black-and-white photos (and maybe a few weeks after that in newsreels).

But their Boomer kids saw the crucial events of their own generation in full sound, color, and commentary, virtually as they were happening, driven by a rock-and-roll soundtrack. Many early Boomers responded to this new national mayhem with civil rights marches, protest songs, and "dropping out." Later, their younger siblings (the late Boomers) opted for the relative calm and comfort of hanging out in the local shopping mall, dancing to disco music, and "selling out" as the *per capita* teenage wealth skyrocketed.

Suburban kids had safe neighborhoods, lots of unearned (by them) money, new technology, freedom of movement, and time to spare. This was the perfect storm for advertisers. The era of "the customer is king" came in like a tsunami. And the church was no exception.

Today, as malls are either adapting to new realities or disappearing entirely, suburban mall-like church facilities are doing the same thing. In an electronically connected world, we are less tethered to geography or architecture than ever. This new analog-to-electronic transition will undoubtedly be the most far-reaching migration ever. With multisite congregations and online options, it no longer matters how many people can fit in a room or how many cars the parking lot can hold, so the size of an individual congregation is virtually limitless. Churches need to be aware of this digital reality. And now we face what's being called the Great De-Churching, with most churches experiencing a significant decline in attendance, and "nones" being the fastest-growing religious demographic.[15] Many pastors and church experts seem to have one of two responses: 1) Get bigger, respond quicker, and find new online ways to reach new people, or 2) go back to what worked in the past, stop offering online church, and emphasize old-fashioned values.

I suggest a third option. Intentionally de-sizing the church.

* * * * *

So, we've looked at the puzzle pieces of 1) the American, church-as-marketplace model, 2) the two streams, how-to-do-it/how-I-did-it church growth models, and 3) the rise of the suburbs and the Boomers. Now we need to see what happened when these forces came together in the church, followed by how to disengage from the problems they've created, and finally, what we can do about it. Those are the subjects of Parts III and IV, starting with the always enticing, ever-present draw toward celebrity to which, unfortunately, the church is not immune.

Part 3

THE CONSEQUENCES OF OUR SIZE OBSESSION

Chapter 7

Inevitable: Why the Christian Celebrity Culture Guarantees Moral Failure

Humans were not fashioned by God for celebrity.
We can't take it, I'm telling you. It's too much.

BETH MOORE

You do not want to be in this chair.
I cannot stress it enough.

CARL LENTZ

For most of us, celebrity and fame feel synonymous. But, while the terms are related, they have distinctions that are not inconsequential. According to Sharon Marcus, the author of *The Drama of Celebrity*, while fame "is a term that's been around since the Romans," it often referred to "great deeds that would be known for millennia." Celebrity is a much newer term and is a "trivial sort of fame that's a flash in the pan."[1] Marcus calls the French actress Sarah Bernhardt the "godmother of modern celebrity."[2] For many years Bernhardt was, by far, the most identifiable person on the planet. Her celebrity

81

was so all-encompassing that even the hard-to-impress Mark Twain quipped, "There are five kinds of actresses: bad actresses, fair actresses, good actresses, great actresses, and Sarah Bernhardt."[3]

Bernhardt was able to become such a phenomenon because her fame corresponded with the arrival of the new technologies of photography, telegraphy, inexpensive printing, and railways— advancements that she cannily embraced and exploited better than anyone else. For the first time in history, one person's image could be made quickly available to (almost) anyone, anywhere. Before these technological advancements, the only people whose images were readily identifiable by the mass population were warriors, rulers, and bygone heroes whose images were seen on statues, coinage, and stamps. What Bernhardt and her modern social media offspring have done is to break through the fame barrier to become public figures in ways that only conquerors and kings had previously been able to do, at speeds they could never have imagined, and for accomplishments that are negligible, at best.

More technology equals more celebrity. They go hand in hand.

The fame of Pharaohs and Caesars took longer to establish, but many of them are still well known millennia later, while Bernhardt, who lived barely a century ago (she died in 1926) is all but forgotten. And so will today's social media stars and celebrity pastors. This is one of the lures and dangers of celebrity, especially in ministry. Today, we can create celebrity in a heartbeat through an online presence. With the internet, anyone—literally anyone—with a device and internet access can become famous for doing nothing other than attracting attention. Skye Jethani noted, "Celebrity pastors are not a new phenomenon, nor is our human tendency to exalt our leaders to unsustainable heights. What is new is the number of celebrity pastors and the speed with which they are being created and corrupted."[4]

What We Celebrate

The size of the audience, whether online or in person, is not an accurate measure of actual impact, value, or permanence. Celebrity, as defined by Katelyn Beaty in *Celebrities for Jesus*, is "social power without proximity."[5] This is a helpful definition. And it clearly places celebrity at odds with the gospel. The gospel is all about laying down power, and the life of the church should create greater proximity—of us to God and to each other. Instead, as Beaty plainly states it, "to have immense social power and little proximity is a spiritually dangerous place to be."[6]

The core of the word "celebrity" is "celebrate." And we imitate what we celebrate. It's inevitable that there will be moral failings within any group of people. But when we elevate leaders through their ability to become celebrities, giving them power over our feelings and decisions while having no genuine proximity in our lives, that celebrity culture always elevates, alienates, then devastates its prey. When you have power but no proximity, you have little to no accountability. And power without accountability always—absolutely *always*—leads to an us/them, have/have-not, rich/poor dynamic that ruins everything it touches.

"Pastoral-ministry celebrity is simply a dangerous thing," wrote Paul David Tripp in *Dangerous Calling*. "Public acclaim is often the seedbed for spiritual pride."[7]

The parasite of size and celebrity always poisons its host. "[Carl Lentz] became his own celebrity," said *The Secrets of Hillsong* docuseries director Stacey Lee. "There was so much murkiness in the mission that the original goals of the church somehow got lost. The goal of this church from the very outset was reaching as many people as possible and, as our religious historian says in the documentary, *in their desire to grow, they never stopped to think if they should.*" Instead, "*rapacious growth had become an end in itself.*"[8]

Fame is not evil, but it is dangerous.

Unfettered growth combined with stratospheric celebrity is a deadly combination, no matter what your original intentions were. You cannot build your brand and develop your spiritual maturity at the same time. They are heading in different directions. That doesn't mean you can't promote your church, an event, or a ministry. But promoting ministry for the betterment of others is very different from promoting your identity for the glorification of self.

On the opposite end of this experience, author Daniel Darling relates how he was grateful for the fame of Timothy Keller.

We often (rightly) critique a relentless pursuit of "platform." But I'm glad there have been faithful Christians with a wide audience because they've made their way to me. If [Tim] Keller isn't published by a mainstream publisher, I don't get to read his works.

And I think this about so many other men and women whose words have helped to shape me. If they were not published in books, or on Christian radio, or in a podcast, or in a magazine article, I'd [sic] never would have had access to their wisdom.

There are so many ways fame can be perverted and can destroy and can be tribal. But there are also so many ways a wide audience can be used for God's glory.[9]

It's okay to accept a bigger platform when it develops naturally, but do not *pursue* bigness. We must reject celebrity and excess, refusing to accommodate or platform those who embrace them. A larger audience can be helpful when it is a necessary tool toward a higher goal, but we can't pursue it for its own sake. Fame is not evil, but it is dangerous.

As Chris Galanos noted, there are consequences when Christians choose a church based on the talent of the pastor:

> This has contributed to a "celebrity preacher" culture in America. And, unfortunately, we're seeing celebrity preachers fall left and right, leaving many people disillusioned. A very famous preacher I've looked up to for years fell into sin and had to step down. It just keeps happening.[10]

Resisting Celebrity

To resist the relentless pull toward celebrity, I suggest four starter steps:

1. Lower the platform
2. Share the platform
3. Leave the platform
4. Remove the platform

First, we need to lower the platform. There are times when one person needs to talk to many people, and we need stages, mics, cameras, and lights to do that. But we must do whatever we can to guard against abuse. Not long ago, I was in a discussion with a group of ministers sharing new ideas when something odd occurred to me. If you took the religious language out of our conversation, I wondered if you'd be able to tell whether we were a group of ministers talking about church or a local theater group talking about the upcoming show season. Much of our discussion focused on issues like stage lighting, how much video or drama to use, the quality and volume of the music, advertising, signage, seating, transitions between segments of the service, and so on. The other voices faded into the background for me, as I realized something about myself: I've spent decades tweaking lights, buying audio equipment, setting up chairs, and all the other work it takes to put on church services. I'm tired of the show.

And it's not just me. This is the message from newer generations, loud and clear, as Skye Jethani writes:

> My generation (Generation X) and Millennials (those born after 1980) have a strong aversion to institutions, and the bigger the institutions, the more distrustful we are. . . . For Boomers large meant legitimate. *If a church is big,* they reasoned, *it must be doing something right,* [but] for younger Americans, big doesn't mean legitimate; big means corrupt.[11]

Previous generations were impressed by the big church stage. The higher the better, both physically and metaphorically. Upcoming generations see the forced distance created by higher platforms as a negative, not a positive. We need to lower the platforms physically, but even more importantly, we need to de-elevate them by removing the relational distance between those who serve onstage and those who serve behind the scenes. As K. J. Ramsey reminds us, "Our real Good Shepherd doesn't stand apart on stages. Our true Good Shepherd holds dirty feet in his God-hands and asks us to let him love us down to the dirt under our toenails."[12]

Second, we should always share the platform. Two of today's healthiest big-church trends are the preaching team and rotating worship leaders. When a congregation rotates the speakers from Sunday to Sunday, and the worship team allows two or three different singers to take the lead in a worship set, it widens the spotlight and reduces (but does not eliminate) the likelihood that one leader will rise to celebrity status. The same thing happens in small churches when they have different members read the Scripture of the day, lead in the serving of communion, and so on.

Third, we need to leave the platform regularly. In the leadership classic *In Search of Excellence*, Tom Peters introduced MBWA, or

Management By Walking Around.[13] Peters explained that too many managers spend all their time in ivory tower offices where they can quickly lose the sense of what's happening on the factory floor. Pastors lose touch when we spend most of our pre- and post-service time in our office or green room instead of walking through the seats and hanging out in the church lobby.

Finally, some platforms need to be removed entirely. Strip them down and burn them, leaving nothing but a smoldering crater where they once stood. Platforms that have been built on celebrity, that have enabled predators, that have abandoned core theology, or that have diverted our attention from the toxic cultures they've been hiding cannot be fixed. They must be destroyed.

Les McKeown calls the last phase of a dying organization the Death Rattle. This is when a church or organization knows they're as good as dead. Right before the Death Rattle is a point of no return that McKeown calls the Big Rut, which is the last desperate chance to salvage anything of value. "You cannot fix an organization in the Big Rut. You can't. What you can do is break the organization up into many, many small pieces," says McKeown. "So long as the senior management all go, that gives the opportunity to restart the other side of the life cycle."[14] Some organizations are so toxic, so dangerous, and have caused so much damage that there is no way to turn them around, no matter how hard you try. Maybe they're in the Big Rut, where they can be sold off for parts using some assets in another organization for God's glory and the healing of the victims. But many are in the Death Rattle. In that final phase, the rot is so embedded that any attempts at salvage will only spread the sickness to another organization.

The Christian celebrity culture is in its death rattle. Sure, it will keep rattling. But it cannot be rescued. "Power has a way of ruining people," wrote McKnight and Barringer. "Success has a way of turning ministers into celebrities. Therefore, pastors must resist the pull toward celebrity."[15]

Chapter 8

What the Church Growth Movement Got Right

*Church growth is discovering more than new
methods: it is discovering the power behind the
principles and methods.*

THOM S. RAINER

L ike the suburbs, megachurches are an easy punching bag. Too easy.
As the poster children for CGM, they bear almost all the burden
for what the movement got wrong, and not nearly enough credit for
what they've done well. Certainly, with the recent advent of numerous articles, books, and documentaries about spectacular megachurch
failures, we know they are not without significant faults. But CGM
isn't just about megachurches, and the news about both isn't all bad.

In the well-researched and practical book *High on God: How
Megachurches Won the Heart of America*, the British authors describe
how their original biases against megachurches were upended when
they not only studied but experienced them firsthand:

> Early on, we thought we'd show their superficiality and
> their biases, and the way they anesthetize churchgoers from
> reality. But then, as we went over the data and continued

attending megachurch services, we began to realize that these are very successful human groups, developing communities that enjoy forms of ecstatic worship, nurture families in positive and joy-filled habits of service and mutual care, and reach out into their communities to offer care, love, and forgiveness as well as food, shelter, and medical relief to those in great need both near and far.[1]

It is my hope to do something similar. To see what's good about a movement that is so easy to demonize, while also taking an honest but fair look at its downsides. First, the good.

CGM emphasized the importance of the local church

I love CGM for doing this. The local church has my heart. I believe it is central to the heart of Jesus and to His plan for the redemption of all creation back to Himself. Even when CGM has gone wrong, it has seldom strayed from an emphasis on the local church. For this, I am profoundly grateful.

CGM emphasized the importance of the global church

One of the reasons for the decline in the importance of denominations over the last couple generations has been the rise of CGM. Since neither of its streams came from a denominational source, many of its proponents have stepped outside their own denominational spheres. While denominations have value (I and my church are part of one), the cross-denominational emphasis of CGM is a positive step toward

> **The cross-denominational emphasis of CGM is a positive step toward greater unity across denominational lines.**

greater unity across denominational lines, often relegating secondary theological issues to the back shelf.

CGM infused the church with some much needed energy

The rise of CGM was an exciting time to be in pastoral ministry. It seemed like every day there was a new book, a new idea, and a new church that was setting a vibrant example of growth that we could follow. The earliest proponents of CGM faced a lot of resistance from churches and pastors. Some of that was active, but most of it was passive; they weren't opposed as much as they didn't seem to care. No one is passive now, and CGM deserves at least some of the credit for awakening church leaders from their lethargy.

CGM introduced new methods of research, assessment, and measurement

Before CGM, a church was considered successful if it *felt* like it was successful. CGM helped us understand the value of quantifiable results. Over the last forty-plus years we have seen an explosion in the number of useful mechanisms for more accurately assessing a congregation's health and effectiveness.

CGM had more academic rigor than it received credit for

As we've already seen, the most dominant names in CGM, including Donald McGavran, the Fuller Church Growth Institute, the Barna Institute, and others, were very concerned with accurate assessments and the applied sciences. We have a lot to learn. Proper research tools, peer-reviewed studies, and an openness to ask hard questions are essential. CGM has done this better than almost any other aspect of church life.

CGM inspired a wealth of shared information

Before CGM, every denomination created, produced, and kept their own ideas and products to themselves. CGM cracked that door open much wider than anyone could have anticipated. Now, even material that is produced from within denominational walls is readily shared with other groups. Nondenominational megachurches and mega-sized parachurch organizations are even more willing to share their discoveries with others through blogs, podcasts, books, conferences, and more. The generosity of shared information is one of the great legacies of CGM.

CGM reminded us to look outside the church walls

Both the American and McGavran CGM streams had a major em-phasis on evangelism. In both movements, it wasn't enough just to care for the people who were already inside the walls. Jesus' empha-sis on the Great Commission has taken center stage throughout the entire history of CGM.

CGM inspired a lot of church planting

Some of the early stats to come from CGM showed us how church planting was like rocket fuel to turbocharge the church. In the 1990s–2000s, we were inundated with information about how many more people came to faith, volunteered, gave generously, and invited their friends when engaged in planting a church, in contrast to at-tending an existing church. This church planting boom was, and remains, an inspiration.

CGM reminded us to focus on the mission

For a decade or more, "missional" became a byword. I remember sit-ting in a conference in the 1990s with a friend who wasn't well-read on the latest church trends. It seemed like every speaker who came up referred to the need for the church to be more missional. During a break, my friend sheepishly asked me, "What does missional actu-ally mean?" When I told him it means what he probably thought it means, to have a mindset of looking outside the walls of the church rather than just inward, his response was, "So it's the Great Commission." "Yes," I said. "Okay. Good to hear it's coming back," he said casually, before taking another bite of his Chick-fil-A sandwich. "I never knew it had left."

CGM expressed an openness to change on extrabiblical methods

This may be one of the most well-known and most criticized aspects of CGM. Church growth proponents loved new methods, systems, programs, and ideas. If they didn't violate core biblical beliefs (or what each church considered to be core beliefs), any idea was fair game. The overall emphasis on seeking new methods, language, and ideas with which to frame the age-old gospel message has been refreshing.

CGM held surprisingly strong on core Bible principles

One of the main concerns about churches adopting new methods and ideas was the slippery slope argument. If you give in on church names, décor, stage design, and so on, the next thing you know you'll be giving in on essential biblical truths—or so went the argument. This prediction has shown itself to be almost 180 degrees off. Today, the churches that were all-in for cosmetic and systemic changes are far more likely to have held firm to traditional biblical beliefs than churches that insisted on keeping traditional formats.

Scott Thumma notes, "Nearly all megachurches have a conservative theological orientation. An overwhelming majority would be considered Evangelical, Charismatic, or Fundamentalist. Even the megachurches from moderate and liberal denominations often stand out as having a more conservative theology than do their counterparts."[2]

CGM emphasized contextualized ministry

"Pay attention to how your neighborhood is changing" was one of the rallying cries of CGM. Like missionaries to a foreign field, local churches were encouraged to speak God's truth in the language of their neighborhoods, not just the insider lingo of the church.

Occasionally this led some pastors to follow certain trends almost comically. For a while it seemed like every church stage featured the speaker wearing skinny jeans and sitting on a stool next to a bar table against a backdrop of wood pallets. Currently, the trend is the flat black wall behind the stage. But for the most part the changes were motivated by a desire for contextualized ministry—speaking the truth of the Scriptures in the language of their neighborhood.

CGM asked hard questions

CGM encouraged church leaders not to settle for business as usual. It asked and demanded hard questions. One of Donald McGavran's lessons that CGM seldom strayed from was to stay laser-focused on proper assessment of what was and was not effective. And it didn't just point its finger outward—it has generally expressed a willingness to receive wounds from a friend.

CGM expressed a willingness to be critiqued

In most areas of theology and church life, any challenge to the status quo is looked upon as divisive at best, and heresy at worst. Not so for most CGM proponents. I don't know of any other church discipline that is more open to hearing and learning from their critics. Which is good, because here goes.

Buckle up. It's a *lot*.

Chapter 9

Where the Church Growth Movement Went Sideways

*In the first twenty years of the movement,
research focused on principles; lately the focus
has been on discovering new techniques,
programs, or methods.*

Elmer Towns

M egachurches and the Church Growth Movement have more than their share of detractors. But I'm not one of them. I have learned some great lessons from all aspects of CGM, from its pioneers, like Donald McGavran, to its best-known practitioners, like Rick Warren. But CGM has a dark side. Many people, including me, have experienced it, but very few have been able to talk about it in healthy, helpful ways. As a disclaimer, I admit that while I learned a lot from CGM, I haven't been very successful at numerical church growth myself. I outlined that in *The Grasshopper Myth*, so I won't retell my story here, except to say that despite living in one of the havens of megachurch mega-growth (Orange County, California) for over thirty years, I never saw the kind of church growth that was expected. So, I had to rethink, recast, and reimagine what a successful church looks like.

Elmer Towns, the cofounder of Liberty University and author of over seventy-five books, believes that criticisms of CGM, while not always accurate, should be taken seriously.[1] He wrote: "The Church Growth movement cannot ignore these criticisms. While they come from well-meaning, yet at times self-serving, sources, these criticisms should only sharpen the focus of those in the movement to do a better job of carrying out the Great Commission."[2] I have no desire to pile on, and I am well-meaning, but hopefully not self-serving. And my concern is not with CGM, but with what it has become since it made its way into the mainstream in the 1990s.

CGM can be a false summit

In his riveting book *Into Thin Air*, Jon Krakauer tells the first-person true story of the 1996 Mount Everest climb that went horribly wrong, becoming the mountain's deadliest season at the time.[3] One of the challenges Krakauer writes vividly about is Everest's false summit. Every climber is told endlessly about this, yet many still fall to its deception. When they arrive at the false summit, they're so discouraged at how far away the actual peak is that they collapse mentally and emotionally. It's one of Everest's many serious dangers.

Church growth has false summits as well. Numerical goals, comparison, annual targets, and more all act as summits that we're sure will satisfy us once we get there, only to give way to yet another, bigger summit ahead. It's a never-ending quest. "Church leaders are especially susceptible to pursuing false summits. In fact, the prevailing scorecard for success in the U.S. Church is a false summit," writes Todd Wilson. "Embracing the right personal scorecard will require surrender. Quite possibly very difficult surrender that requires you to deal with some impure motives and heart conditions."[4]

Numerical church growth is not a goal; it's a by-product. When we see bigness as a goal, it becomes a false summit and a dangerous deception. "I've always harbored more than a few concerns about church growth being just a numbers game," writes Gary McIntosh. "If growth were the destination, we would have a clear target size given in Scripture. God surely would have told us how big he wants churches to get. He would have instructed us when to stop growing at a

> **When we see bigness as a goal, it becomes a false summit and a dangerous deception.**

certain size or when to spin off a new congregation."[5] But Jesus didn't do that because "bigger" is not a goal, it's a false summit. Don't let it fool you.

CGM often emphasized numerical growth over discipleship

Donald McGavran was obsessed with discipleship and people movements, but much of today's church growth teaching emphasizes crowd size, exclusively. Todd Wilson again writes, "We measure the things that fuel our lust for addition growth and accumulating rather than the disciple makers who fuel multiplication."[6] This is not universal in growing churches, of course (none of these negatives are universal), but it's far too prevalent.

CGM got sidelined by vision statement obsession

"I'm afraid that I don't have much truck [I'm not on board] with the 'vision statements' that seem to fuel the ambition of pastors these days," wrote Eugene Petersen in 2008.[7]

Anyone who pastored in the late 1990s–2000s heard a lot about the need for every church to have a clear vision statement. If you pastored then, you may have attended workshops to help your church create one. Since almost every survey of fast-growing megachurches showed that they all had a clear, memorable vision statement, the assumption was that mission statements were one of the reasons these churches grew to mega size. But most churches who tried that path to growth found it wanting. This too was a false summit.

Mission, vision, and purpose statements were terms that were used to describe a memorable sentence of twelve words or less that a pastor or church leadership team would create to describe the manner in which they planned to fulfill God's mission for the church. While many churches used rhymes (Know, Grow, and Go) or acronyms (Jesus, Others, You), perhaps the most well-known one from that era was Willow Creek's hopeful statement, "To turn irreligious people into fully devoted followers of Christ."[8]

While some church leaders went to great lengths to distinguish the differences between mission, vision, and purpose statements, there was never any widespread agreement about what those differences were, so most pastors used them interchangeably, which I will do as well.

First, the mission statement was never meant to be a one-step fix. It wasn't presented that way, even by its most avid proponents. But the drive to craft a compelling mission statement was so relentless that most pastors made the leap from "this is an ingredient toward growth" to "this is the magic bullet for growth." It was neither.

Second, we had the order of cause/effect wrong. Rather than vision statements creating megachurches, megachurches created the need for vision statements. When a church is small, the vision and mission tend to be communicated organically and relationally. Not sure what to do next? Just ask the pastor or a deacon, they're likely in the room, planning the event alongside you. But as a church gets bigger, the pastor and other staff-level leaders are absent for most of the church's events and department-level planning sessions. So, you rely on the mission statement. When a church gets bigger, the mission statement is a stand-in for the physical presence of church leaders. Large churches create mission statements, but there's no evidence that mission statements create large churches.

CGM can fall prey to methodology worship

Better methods are important. If we can improve, we should. But better methodology is not the answer to our problems. Jesus is. Church leaders regularly propose that methods aren't sacred, with sayings like "Methods are many, but principles are few. Methods always change. Principles never do."[9]

Andy Stanley wrote, "Marry your mission. Date your model (method). Fall in love with your vision. Stay mildly infatuated with your approach."[10] I fully agree. But I don't think Stanley would have felt compelled to say that—and others would not have quoted him so often on it—if methodology worship wasn't such a problem. But here's what we may be missing. The primary target of every "don't marry the method" teaching I've heard is to convince older, smaller churches that their stale methods should be changed. And that's often true. But in our pushback against stale methods, we've swung the pendulum too far. In many churches, the danger isn't that we're enamored with old models, but that we've become obsessed to the point of idolatry with the newest idea. Francis Chan found himself in exactly that place: "For decades church leaders like me have lost sight of the powerful mystery inherent in the Church and have instead run to other methods to keep people interested."[11] Whether it's being married to the old method or obsessed with chasing the newer model, methodology worship is an ever-present problem.

> **In many churches, the danger isn't that we're enamored with old models, but that we've become obsessed to the point of idolatry with the newest idea.**

CGM used numbers as the proof that the church is healthy

In the article "10 Dangerous Myths About Church Growth," Brian Orme addresses the myth that "The More You Grow, the Healthier You Are." He writes, "Health deals more with what's going on below the surface. Growth tells us something's going on, but whether it's good or bad, that's another issue."[12] I love the way he phrases that. Growth is certainly an indicator that *something* is going on, but what that something is requires a lot more research than numbers on a spreadsheet. The ever-present danger is that we see the numbers as an indication to look no further when it should be causing us to look deeper. "Because it's big" can no longer be an acceptable answer to the question "How do I know this church is doing well?"

Perhaps we can take a page from major league sports for this. In 1998, Mark McGwire and Sammy Sosa were largely credited with "saving baseball" when their race to eclipse Roger Maris's home run record captured the world's attention. Enormous blasts, fueled by their massive physiques, seemed to prove that bigger is certainly better. But it all came crashing down quickly in the 2000s when doping scandals exposed so many athletes for taking performance-enhancing drugs. The accused players included McGwire and Sosa, along with Barry Bonds who had broken McGwire's record in 2001. Today, those players are not primarily remembered for their home runs, but for the scandals that have so tainted them that none of them are in the Baseball Hall of Fame, nor are they ever likely to be.

The parallels from baseball to megachurch scandals are so strong, they're almost spooky. Bigger doesn't always mean healthier.

CGM can be a breeding ground for toxic positivity

Optimism is an essential element in leadership. As followers of Jesus, we have the ultimate reason to be optimistic because we know that Jesus is working all things for the good of those who love God and are called according to His purpose.[13] But that optimism becomes toxic when it refuses to acknowledge any negative realities whatsoever. *Psychology Today* describes toxic positivity as "the act of avoiding, suppressing, or rejecting negative emotions or experiences. This may take the form of denying your own emotions or someone else denying your emotions, insisting on positive thinking instead."[14]

When Christians exhibit toxic positivity, they jump to "Be of good cheer, I have overcome the world," without acknowledging that the first half of that verse is "In the world you will have tribulation."[15] In CGM, there has been a tendency to celebrate the positives (which we should do) while ignoring or suppressing the negatives (which is dangerous to do). This is done in the name of faith. But biblical faith doesn't deny the negatives. The resurrection of Jesus is the foundation of everything we believe, but that glorious moment could not have happened without the crucifixion. Faith doesn't shrink from acknowledging difficulties, sins, or failures; it faces them head-on.

CGM's numerical obsession can blind us to deeper truths

When the numbers stay up, they capture our attention, blinding us to what might really be going on in the church, including in the pastor's own walk with God. If all healthy things grow, the assumption is that all church growth is healthy. Because of this false equivalency, increasing numbers can cause us to make two equal but opposite mistakes about church growth and church health. While decreasing numbers cause us to look deeper for problems, increasing numbers can cause us to ignore the cancer in an unhealthy church because we're blinded by the positives on the surface. Also, static attendance numbers can often cause church leaders to miss the wonderful ministry happening in a healthy church. We can't ignore numbers, but we should take care not to depend on them so much that they blind us to the non-numerical realities of spiritual and emotional health.

CGM created winners and losers . . .

. . . mostly losers. Even though nobody uses the term, that's how it often feels. Think of all the stats saying that up to 90 percent of churches are stalled or failing. Now, put yourself in the shoes of the 90 percent (if you aren't in those shoes already, which is highly likely). That's what "loser" feels like. And it doesn't seem to matter how well the church is fulfilling its mission in other ways. If the numbers aren't up, it feels like losing. Too many pastors of healthy small churches live in frustration and self-loathing, not because the church isn't doing well, but because the numbers aren't increasing like so many post-CGM principles tell us is inevitable.

"While the movement has brought numerical increase for some churches, it has also generated frustrations and feelings of failure for those who do not experience the same results," notes Dave Beckwith. "I still see pastors put out to pasture simply because attendance isn't steadily increasing."[16]

CGM platformed pastors of growing churches almost exclusively

When was the last time you saw the pastor of a small, but healthy, church being promoted as the headline speaker at a church leadership conference? Yes, it's happened, but it's rare enough that most pastors have never seen it. We can learn a lot from pastors whose churches are experiencing rapid growth, but that's not the only direction the wisdom can flow. When we constantly elevate numerical growth almost exclusively, we devalue the importance of the simple, faithful ministry that most pastors and churches are called to do.

CGM created an unrealistic burden on pastors

I love pastors. I am one, and I was raised by one, who was also raised by one (if you're counting, that makes me a third-generation pastor). But the post-CGM church has exhibited an obsession with pastors of fast-growing churches, as if they possessed near mythical powers.

In the middle of the CGM boom of the 1980s and '90s, one church growth proponent acknowledged that "in America, the primary catalytic factor for growth in a local church is the pastor. In every growing, dynamic church I have studied, I have found a key person whom God is using to make it happen."[17] Another emphasized that in American churches, the focus on the strong, entrepreneurial pastor is "a central church growth principle."[18]

Not only did this hyper-focus on the pastor contribute to the unhealthy celebrity culture, but it also continues to create a burden on pastors that we're not built to sustain.

CGM emphasized speed over depth

Look at how speakers and their churches are promoted at almost every conference. It's not just about how big their church is or how much they're growing, but how quickly it's happening. It's not enough to say "their church increased from 30 to 3,000!" It has to be "their church increased from 30 to 3,000 *in just three years!*" The speed has become as important as the size. And both are promoted far more often than the growth in spiritual maturity of the people who were added to the church. "Our culture has conditioned us to expect instant results and overnight success," author Jeff Goins reminds us. "This impatience runs so rampant that we dress it up in terms like 'efficiency' and 'productivity.' But really what's happening is we are conditioning ourselves to get what we want now, all the time."[19]

Metrics can give us fast answers. In fact, the faster the better. But discipleship is slow. Depth doesn't happen overnight. It takes ponderously long amounts of time. But much of the post-CGM church doesn't have the patience for that. This often means that good pastors aren't always given the time they need to grow roots deeply. That creates even further levels of stress and unrest, which (ironically) stifle long-term numerical growth. "Healthy churches don't typically grow by leaps and bounds, through splashy initiatives and clever strategies," notes pastor Gunner Gundersen. "They grow like trees—slow, steady, strong, with small but certain rings to show for each passing year of faithful collective ministry."[20]

CGM devalued current strengths for future expectations

Since the advent of CGM, it's no longer enough for a congregation to be doing vibrant ministry at its current size. You're expected to be actively pursuing bigger, future-oriented goals. Certainly, it's healthy to keep a sense of forward motion in our hearts and our churches. That kind of motivation can be inspiring and encouraging. But we also need to pause, look around, and appreciate what we have here and now.

CGM created churches further divided along racial and economic lines

As mentioned earlier, the American church growth stream took McGavran's idea of a racially homogenous church and twisted it to mean that we only attend church with people who look like us. This has led to even further isolation of churches along racial and economic lines.

For instance, some churches create an avatar of their "target" person. The most well-known is Saddleback Sam, pictured as a busy, young, tech-savvy, white, middle-to-upper-income male. The advantages of such avatars, according to marketing expert Thomas Costello of REACHRIGHT, include "understanding the needs, preferences, and backgrounds of their congregation," "empathy mapping," and "community building."[21]

But, while a church may intend to use an avatar "to create meaningful relationships and foster spiritual growth in the congregation,"[22] when you describe your target as young, white, male, and upper/middle income, it automatically disenfranchises everyone else. You may not mean to, but you can't accept the positives of creating an avatar without acknowledging their downsides, as well.

CGM created larger churches, which created larger dangers

"A fallen small-church pastor is a problem. A fallen megachurch pastor is a disaster," notes Bob Smietana.[23] While small-church pastors are no less likely to have a moral failing than big-church pastors, the spotlight that shines so bright on a big stage can burn nuclear when a big-church pastor falls. The damage caused by the moral failings of a local pastor are devastating to those affected by it, but the circle of injury tends to be local or regional. But the damage caused by the moral failings of a celebrity preacher are often global and are virtually limitless.

CGM created the megachurch focus problem

When we stay focused on big churches, it's easy to think of Christianity through a predominantly white, American lens. But the primary growth of the global church is happening outside of Europe and America. According to Gordon-Conwell University, "In 2000, 62% of Christians globally were of color (1.2 billion). In 2015, 68% of Christians are of color (1.6 billion)." As a subset of overall Christianity, evangelicalism is even more ethnically and racially diverse. "In 2000, 79.1% of all Evangelicals were of color (non-white; 185.2 million). In 2015, 84.1% of all Evangelicals in the world are of color (non-white; 270.1 million)."[24]

In addition, author Howard Snyder writes, "Most church growth historically does not come from huge churches but from small to medium-sized congregations."[25] This shift in global Christian growth—from predominantly white and big-church-focused places to non-white, small-church spaces—is something that church historians and global church-growth experts have been aware of for a long time. American Evangelicalism is still a majority-white and big-church movement, but it is now considered an outlier in the way the church is growing globally.[26]

Gordon-Conwell's data and Snyder's concerns match McGavran's original research and cautions about the American church-growth stream. Big churches are seldom a sign of overall Christian growth. In most cases, their size is a result of consolidation. There aren't necessarily more Christians where megachurches are growing; believers are just gathering in larger groups.

CGM can feel more concerned with big churches than actual church growth

As we saw in the positives, CGM stayed remarkably faithful to the strengthening of the local church. But even that positive emphasis can go to an unhealthy extreme. In the case of CGM, the local church emphasis has been so strong as to be suffocating. Most church growth proponents are almost exclusively focused on one thing: making individual congregations larger. This has now become the very definition of church growth itself. But the only church growth anyone should be concerned about is seeing people come to Christ, getting discipled, and becoming disciple-makers themselves. We can't call it church growth when only a handful of congregations are getting larger while the rest are static or struggling. For the most part, big churches don't happen where Christianity is growing, but where Christians have money. This is not a bad thing, but it's not church growth. We need to think beyond individual congregations. Church growth happens, not when individual churches get bigger, but when Christians are increasing as a percentage of the overall population.

According to Bob Smietana, citing the work of sociologist Mark Chaves of Duke Divinity School, "Rather than the growth of megachurches being a sign of religious vitality, Chaves suspects that it is another sign that organized religion is on the decline."[27] This did not happen in an ecclesiastical vacuum. Smietana explains the part culture has played:

> There is an inequality among religious organizations that mirrors some of the large inequalities in American culture. A relative handful of big churches have about half of the money and people, as Chaves noted. Small churches—which make up the vast majority of congregations in communities across the US—have a shrinking number of people and resources to work with.
>
> And this trend is likely to continue in the future.[28]

CGM contributed to the megachurch variety problem

There seems to be a lot of similarities in style and methodology among megachurches. When you get that big, certain systems simply work across denominational and theological lines. New research is coming in to back up these observations. In the popular 2023 article "There's a Reason Every Hit Worship Song Sounds the Same," Bob Smietana noted that, of the thirty-eight songs in the combined Top 25 from CCLI and PraiseCharts, all but two were from artists associated with four megachurches (Bethel, Passion, Hillsong, and Elevation).[29] The emphasis on what works in megachurches has led to a flattening of church cultures as their ideas, songs, methods, and mindset have filtered down to churches of all sizes and places.

Yet, there are holdouts. In a follow-up article, Smietana interviewed Will Bishop, associate professor of church music and worship at SBTS in Louisville, Kentucky. Bishop notes that while this flattening trend is true, his survey results from 127 churches determined that it's far from universal. His study found that "smaller churches are like the Wild West" musically, where "anything goes,"[30] from traditional to contemporary, hymnbooks to screens, even a smattering of secular favorites. As someone who is regularly in a wide variety of small church worship services, I can confirm that his study matches my experience. I find this very hopeful.

CGM contributed to a dangerous arrogance/shame cycle

When everything has to be measured, we end up comparing ourselves to others. It's inevitable. Measurement *is* comparison. And when we compare the size of our church or ministry to the size of others, we'll find that either we're bigger than they are and be filled with pride, or smaller and be filled with shame. Neither is the basis for a healthy ministry. This cycle plays out in a phenomenon called the Dunning-Kruger Effect.[31] Between 1999 and 2003, David Dunning and Justin Kruger, along with other researchers, performed five different studies that determined people tend to overestimate their skills after learning just a little about a given subject because "their incompetence deprives them of the skills needed to recognize their deficits."[32] This phenomenon has been illustrated in various ways by others, as seen in the following graph, which illustrates this cognitive bias:

THE DUNNING-KRUGER EFFECT [33]

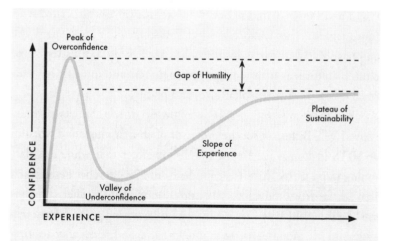

Dunning and Kruger discovered that people often have a ridiculously high degree of confidence (y-axis of graph) about a subject when they first learn a little bit about it. This is often seen in the first-year theology student or the young seminary graduate. They head into ministry supremely confident in their abilities because of their newfound knowledge. This combination of extreme confidence with a small amount of knowledge or experience places them on what I've called the Peak of Overconfidence. This is the arrogance part of the arrogance/shame cycle. This especially happens if a pastor or associate pastor experiences a great deal of numerical success in their first ministry position. Suddenly they're touted as the latest example to follow, which increases their confidence and accompanying arrogance. Because of this, they can sit on the Peak of Overconfidence for a long time, ignoring the wisdom of those with less numerical success but more experience.

But if instead of sitting in arrogance we stay humble and keep learning, we will eventually find ourselves feeling the opposite of arrogance. After the complexities of real-life ministry start kicking in, our confidence may take some hits. Soon we can slip off that mountain and down into the Valley of Underconfidence. This is where the "shame" half kicks in. But we don't have to devolve into shame. If we approach ministry with humility, the fact that we still have a lot to learn can be motivating and invigorating.

Unfortunately, the Valley of Underconfidence is where so many pastors quit ministry and walk away forever. It's not because they're not called. It's usually because they were so overconfident in their own abilities in the first heady years of ministry that the hard, cold slap of real-life pastoral ministry makes them doubt their calling. The sad part is, they stopped too soon. If they'd kept going, they'd have started the long, slow, but rewarding climb up the Slope of Experience, where experience and confidence increase *at the same rate. That* pace is sustainable. But the relentless push for *More! Bigger! Faster!*

doesn't allow it. Instead, it fuels the beast, either keeping people scrambling to stay on top of the Peak of Overconfidence (arrogance when their church grows) or leaving them locked in the Valley of Underconfidence (shame when it doesn't grow).

It seems our CGM mindset throughout the 1990s–2000s kept us on the top of the Peak of Overconfidence. We knew just enough about these new ideas to feel very sure of ourselves. Plus, we could point to churches that were making the principles work. Never mind the vast majority that tried and failed. Today, however, with church attendance rates dropping across the board, and previously growing churches experiencing their first extended downturns following the COVID pandemic lockdowns, many of us are in the middle of the Valley of Underconfidence. This is not bad news. We need to go through this. The decades of high confidence with little understanding about church growth were not sustainable. Now we can step into a more mature stage of experience in which our confidence and experience can grow at the same pace, creating long-term stability and competence, not because of our "own understanding" but in the realization that God will "direct our paths" if we let Him (Prov. 3:5–6 NKJV).

The goal, then, is to keep learning as we move up the Slope of Experience, until we reach the Plateau of Sustainability. At this point, we keep growing, but we never again hit the heights of arrogance that we had at the Peak of Overconfidence. The humility we gain through real-world ministry experience can provide a cushion (the Gap of Humility) that helps us from ever entering the arrogance/shame cycle again.

Church Growth: What's in a Name?

One of the biggest obstacles to overcome in our obsession with numbers is the choice of terms used by McGavran to describe his ideas—namely, Church *Growth*. We referenced why he chose this term back in chapter 3, but we need to address the problems the term has created, as well. Because of the idiosyncrasies of the English language, church growth puts the emphasis on *growth* rather than *church*.

Craig Van Gelder explains the significance of the usage:

> Whenever the word church is used as an adjective to describe something else, the tendency is to place the focus on the function that is being described by the noun—renewal, growth, or effectiveness. . . . Thus, it is more biblical to speak of "the growth of the church" rather than "church growth."[34]

This change of phrasing matters. Our language informs both our theology and our practice of ministry. Thus, the term *church growth* may be one of the primary reasons for our confusion over what the movement was intended to accomplish, and it remains a huge point of misunderstanding. I wish we had a better term. Unfortunately, that ship has sailed. The term is entrenched. So, we need to press on and either reengineer what church growth means to us (an almost impossible task) or abandon the terminology and set our sights on a different trajectory. I'm convinced that the latter is our only reasonable, biblical way forward.

We can't go back to the McGavran river. We're too far downstream for that. But we can learn from it and build on it. Start with prayer. Ask better questions. Learn from the cases of true renewal and revival. Reject stationocracy. Use metrics, but don't be obsessed with individual congregational bigness.

Chapter 10

Beyond the Big/Small Divide

*The megachurches are certainly drawing believers
from other smaller churches, but they are not
putting them out of business. There seems to be
enough growth to go around.*

GLENN T. STANTON

Before automobiles, buggy whips were big business. If you drove a horse-drawn carriage, you needed a buggy whip, and because of the rough use they received, they wore out quickly. Over the centuries, buggy whip manufacturers created better models, which reached their zenith just as the automobile became popular and put the manufacturers out of business. Since then, the buggy whip has become shorthand for an idea that is working exceptionally well but is about to be made redundant by new technology.[1] In the 1990s, the buggy whip was a popular metaphor used by CGM proponents to tell pastors and churches they needed to catch up to new ideas or get left behind. Now, the movement that encouraged us to get rid of the buggy whip then could be today's buggy whip. According to church-planter Peyton Jones, "We've inherited a system that is built on something that no longer works: the church growth movement. . . .

Churches operating under the church growth paradigm are reported by denominational leaders to be over 90 percent in decline."[2]

Today, if you're pushing for a bigger venue, you're promoting a bygone trend. It still has its proponents and successes, but it's yesterday's news. As are big church buildings. I recently asked an architect friend about trends in church facilities. While attendance figures are a lagging indicator (they can only tell you about events that have already happened), architecture is a leading indicator. Because of the advance planning needed, and the necessity of designing facilities that will last for decades, church building design needs to stay way ahead of trends, anticipating where things are going as best they can. One of the leading trends is that no one is building the massive meeting place where everyone worships in the same place at the same time anymore. And they won't be doing so for decades. It's all about multisite, multi-service times, and mix-and-match pods. The biggest churches in the world are discovering that a whole lot of small works better. As Skye Jethani noted, "The construction of larger church buildings is at an all-time low in the United States—a trend that started well before the Great Recession."[3]

So, if you're still using phrases like "all healthy things grow," you're behind the curve on church leadership. Like the buggy whip, obsession over attendance is nothing new. Those who are old enough will remember the days of the wooden sign at the front of the church that showed the attendance and offerings for last week, last year, and year-to-date. Many denominations in that era made pins and ribbons for perfect attendance that were worn proudly on people's suits and dresses like military honors.

An obsession with church attendance has been with us for a long time. But it's become a bigger deal in the last generation or so for one reason: we've become really good at tracking every aspect of it. Instead of using a wooden sign with changeable letters and numbers, we now use spreadsheets, apps, and automatically generated year-to-year comparisons of everything from attendance figures to offerings, small group percentages, and more. Someday we'll look back at today's "fastest-growing churches" lists the way we currently reminisce about ribbons for perfect attendance—as sincere but misguided attempts to measure church success. Nevertheless, the gap between big churches and small churches is wider than ever. Here's why.

The Origin of the Big/Small Divide

The size of the average American church is dropping. In 2000, the average church attendance was 137. By 2020 (but pre-pandemic), it had dropped to 65.[4] Meanwhile, as we saw in chapter 6, the number of megachurches is doubling every decade. The big are getting bigger, while the small are getting smaller. But that's just one way to consider the growth gap. Here's another.

In the 1960s–70s, most large American cities not only didn't have a megachurch (as we've seen, there were only 16 of them in 1969) but the biggest church in a large, well-churched city was often under 1,000. That was a maximum of thirteen or fourteen times the average size of 75. Today, the typical American church is 65, while the biggest church in a large city is often 6,500, 10,000, and upwards. That's *100 to 200 times* the average size. This is no longer just a numerical gap. This creates a massive distance in systems, methods, perceptions, and more.

In the 1960s–70s, if you attended the largest church in town on one Sunday, then visited an average-sized church of 75 of the same denomination the next week, they would both likely be singing from the same hymnbooks; using the same programs for kids, youth, men, and women; supporting the same missionaries; and so on. The only difference might be that one had a bigger choir and some full-time staff. Not anymore. Today, the biggest church in town is almost certainly nondenominational; but even if the biggest church and an average-sized church are the same denomination, that's likely where the obvious similarities end. As the biggest churches have become more massive, they have developed entirely new methods and systems that correspond to their enormous size. Then, when they learn these new methods, they share them with everyone. Mid-size to large churches—even ones that are ten times smaller—use these methods readily because what works in a church of 6,500 can usually be adapted for a church of 650, just drop a zero. But when a typical-sized church of 65 tries to use those methods, they fall flat, and the average pastor feels like a failure, again. It's not because the pastor of a church of 65 isn't capable, or because the methods from a church of 6,500 are wrong, but because dropping two zeroes doesn't work. The size gap is too vast. So, the divide gets bigger, not just between the average-sized church and the megachurch, but between the average-sized church and the mid-sized to big churches that adapted megachurch principles.

The impact of the megachurch cannot be overstated. While there are adamant voices saying that this change is good, and just as many saying it's bad, my take is that this is a significant but lateral move. There's no evidence that megachurches and their pastors are any better or worse an influence on Christianity than the previous influencers, like denominational leaders and crusading reformers. Either way, their impact must be recognized and assessed. And the results must be subject to rigorous, but fair, criticism.

A Tale of Four Churches

Imagine two sets of churches. We'll call the first set Church One and Church Two. Church One is growing numerically, their year-to-year metrics are overwhelmingly positive. The pastor is asked to speak and write about church growth. Their consistent numerical increase is seen as evidence that they're doing the right thing and God is blessing their efforts.

Behind the scenes, there's a busyness bordering on frantic. Everyone puts in 60–70 hours a week, and they very seldom take days off, but the excitement of growth and the drive for more is like a drug that pushes them and keeps them motivated. Mostly. The pastor and some staff members are having family issues because of frequent absences from home and relational disconnect when they are home. Some are medicating their emotional needs with an overuse of stimulants. One is having a secret relationship that crosses emotional and relational boundaries. On the surface, life couldn't be better. Beneath the surface, cracks are forming. But everyone assures themselves that the cracks are minor and temporary. It's a busy season. That's the price of growth. It will slow down soon. The next level of growth will be easier.

Church Two is experiencing something quite different. No matter what they do, they can't get the numbers up. People seem to like the church. The core team feels like they're doing good ministry. But no matter how closely they follow church growth strategies, they can't get past a numerical plateau. They're stuck. This frustration is producing the same kinds of emotional cracks behind the scenes that Church One is experiencing. The long hours, family neglect, self-medicating, lack of emotional and relational boundaries look suspiciously like Church One, but the numerical results are very different. The pastor contemplates leaving.

To an outside observer, these two churches are in opposite places. Church One is seen as an example of how to do ministry well. Church Two must be doing something wrong. But both churches have the same problem. They're chasing bigness. Their obsession with numerical growth is producing very different external results, but it's creating the same internal problems. Like the Ephesian church in Revelation 2, they've lost their first love. In Church One, their numerical success is hiding their problems from them. *The underlying stress can't be that bad*, they think. *God wouldn't be blessing us like this if it was.*

Meanwhile, Church Two doesn't see their internal problems either, because their lack of external success overwhelms them. *Our lack of attendance is the problem,* they think. *If we can get the numbers right, everything else will be okay.*

Thankfully, those aren't our only options. Let's look at the second set: Churches A and B.

Church A is large and has long-term sustained growth, built on the slow, steady process of worship, discipleship, and real-world ministry. They have the occasional down year numerically, but instead of pushing for numbers, the church leaders are always asking *What is Jesus calling us to do and be? How faithfully are we doing it?* and *How is your soul?* Pastoral staff and volunteers are encouraged, even required, to take regular days off and extended vacations.

Church B is small, vibrant, and doing great work in and outside the church walls. Their services are worshipful, their fellowship is close, their ministry lifts people up. People are coming to Christ, being discipled, and sent out into ministry. The pastor and volunteers are focused on reaching their community. They have the occasional discussion about why they aren't growing numerically, but it's not the main topic of conversation. They know they have more to learn, and they're eager to learn it. There are days when the pastor turns off the phone and is unavailable to anyone but the family. And everyone is okay with that because they know how important it is. Plus, there's a deacon who's available to take emergency calls.

From the outside, most people would say Churches One and A are similar since they're both growing numerically. Likewise, most people would say that churches Two and B are similar because they're both numerically "stuck." But churches One and Two have far more in common than their numerical differences would indicate, as do churches A and B.

For a couple of generations, we've had a linear view of church health and size. We put small on the unhealthy side, and place big (or numerically growing) on the healthy side. With a bigger-is-better mindset, we start with the assumption that small means unhealthy, while large and growing means healthy.

A LINEAR VIEW OF SIZE AND HEALTH

SMALL   **BIG**

(Presumed Unhealthy)   (Presumed Healthy)

In most assessments of church health and effectiveness, we don't start by looking at healthy churches of all sizes, we start by looking at the biggest, fast-growing ones and asking, "How did they get there?" Whatever those fast-growing churches are doing becomes the standard for what every church *should* do. But we seldom ask, "What's really going on in the church we're following and learning from? Are they Church One, growing on the outside but rotting from the inside, or are they Church A, growing on a solid footing?" Meanwhile, the lessons that could be learned from small but healthy and missional Church B aren't even considered because they're not "winning" the numbers contest.

This is due to a phenomenon called "survivorship bias," which is the tendency to assume that, because a person, group, or other entity survived, succeeded, or "won," they obviously did everything right. Meanwhile, those who "lost" or didn't survive apparently did everything wrong. This is what happens after a sporting event. Two teams might have equal scores through the end of regulation and into overtime, but as soon as one team scores the winning goal, run, or basket, the commentators start talking about everything the winning team did right and everything the losing team did wrong. That's survivorship bias. We assume the best of those that won, while assuming the worst of those that lost. And in too many church leadership circles, big and growing means winning, while small and numerically steady means losing.

According to Tod Bolsinger in *Canoeing the Mountains*, "Survivorship bias is not only what makes us believe in the quick fixes, [it's also] what makes a church leadership council believe that to attract young adults to their church they should never have a worship leader who is over thirty (true story, sadly!), or to mimic the success of the megachurch down the street (who has a completely different code). It is also what makes us eliminate voices we have marginalized."[5]

One of the first steps in de-sizing the church is to challenge this linear, one-dimensional view of church health and size by expanding our vision (literally and figuratively) into a two-dimensional model that shows church health and size as different. In this Expanded View of Size and Health (pictured below), we make room for all four to be represented far more accurately. In this model, we're less likely to fall into incorrect assumptions about their health and value.

EXPANDED VIEW OF SIZE AND HEALTH

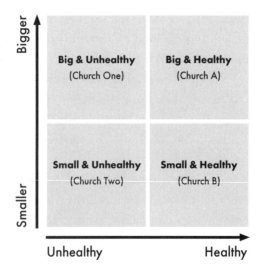

120

Instead of seeing the smaller churches as failures and the bigger churches as successes, we see that the healthier churches of both sizes are those we should learn from, while the unhealthy churches of both sizes have more work to do.

Certainly, the big unhealthy church is likely to learn more from the big healthy church. But it's also true that the small unhealthy church can probably learn more from the small healthy church than from either of the big churches. Either way, the advice needs to flow horizontally, from healthy to unhealthy (no matter the size) rather than vertically, from big to small (no matter the health).

Getting obsessed with bigness doesn't necessarily mean we have impure motives. It often starts because of a pursuit of good things. It did for me. I wasn't running after bigger attendance numbers for

We must not succumb to the tyranny of results.

ego (at least, not consciously) but because I truly wanted to serve Jesus and His church, and almost every voice was telling me that being faithful would produce tangible, numerical growth. And if it didn't result in rising numbers, maybe I wasn't being as faithful as I wanted to be.

It's hard to say this, but pure motives are not enough. The challenge with starting our numbers obsession with a righteous motivation is that it soon becomes a justification. Before we know it, we're excusing all sorts of questionable behavior because we believe it's still based on those original pure motivations, even if they have long since morphed into something far more ego-driven than kingdom-minded. Bigness is a powerful drug. And, like all drugs, our system demands more of it to maintain the original high.

We must not succumb to the tyranny of results.

Numbers Are Not People

You might now be asking a couple important questions, including "What's wrong with following the numbers?" and "Every number is a person, isn't it?"

The simple answer is *no*. People are not numbers and numbers are not people. It's true that every time you type an attendance number onto a spreadsheet, those numbers represent people. But the key word in that sentence is *represent*. Those numbers *represent* people, but a representation of the thing is, by definition, *not* the thing itself. That's the very purpose of the numbers—to reduce the actual people to a quickly identifiable, portable, and workable number for use in planning, programming, and organizing. In his article "Measure what you care about (re: the big sign over your desk)," Seth Godin, a marketing expert and master of the no-caps-in-the-title mini-blog, wrote, "Sometimes, the thing that matters doesn't make it easy for you to measure it. The easiest path is to find a stand-in for what you care about and measure that instead."[6]

Neither Godin nor I are against using numbers. Counting has to be done; attendance has to be taken. But we all must recognize that numbers are, at best, a proxy for actual people. The moment you transfer the people in the room onto a spreadsheet, they're not people anymore—no more than a person's online avatar is that person. When we substitute numbers for people, we depersonalize them. Yes, it's more efficient, simple, and manageable, but it's also *less than*. Engaging with numbers is not engaging with people. We have to stop telling ourselves it is. Raw numbers allow for tracking and organizing, but it's important to recognize that numbers have limitations.

Here are a few of those limitations:

First, numbers are not solutions. Knowing how many people attended an event doesn't fix anything. Seeing a 15 percent drop on a spreadsheet doesn't tell you how to reverse the decline. Numbers inform, but they don't solve anything on their own.

Second, numbers are not objective. We think they are, but we know they're not. Despite sayings like "the numbers don't lie," we all know they can. Numbers are regularly manipulated to mean whatever the user wants them to mean.

Third, numbers can deceive us into thinking we know more than we do. It's too easy to convince ourselves that we know about a church, a cause, or a group of people because we pored over survey results and demographic studies. Plus, while you may gain some understanding of a large group through studying trends and metadata, when the group is small, numbers are less helpful. They can even be misleading. For instance, there's a popular principle that your values are reflected in your budget, so you can tell if a church is reaching the needy people in their community by how much of their budget they allocate for charitable work. In a big church, this financial metric might be an accurate reflection of their commitment, but many small churches are doing massively helpful community work entirely off-book through donations of time, skills, and other resources.

The only way to get accurate information from small groups of people is to spend face-to-face time with them. Them. Not their representative numbers.

Fourth, we don't count what matters, we count what's countable.[7] Love can't be counted. Eternity can't be counted. Neither can joy, salvation, hope, worship, or any of the central aspects of our faith. So, we use numbers as a proxy for the things that really matter. This is fine if we do two things: 1) acknowledge that they're just a proxy, not the real thing, and 2) keep our focus on the non-quantifiable essentials.

Fifth, how much of our desire to measure everything is actually about our need to control, disguised as a passion for growth?

Measuring is a form of naming, and naming is about control. You name what you own. But we don't own the church.

Sixth, it's a very short step from using numbers as a measure to using them as a justification. "You can't argue with success," goes yet another old saying. But you can. And you should. Numerical success does not equal moral rightness. They don't have to be in conflict, but they're not the same thing. Yet, it's too easy to believe that God is blessing what the church is doing if the numbers are increasing.

Seventh, numbers are transactional. As we saw in the word cloud from my Economics 101 class, it's hard, if not impossible, to think about everything numerically without filtering it through the lens of an exchange of goods and services. Gregg Allison and Bryce Butler warn us: "Whatever the pros and cons of this style in business, we believe a transactional leadership culture is fundamentally wrong in the church."[8] This transactional aspect of numbers is what causes us to refer to people with terms like "giving units." (Makes me queasy every time I hear it.)

Eighth, the act of counting has unforeseeable consequences. According to Heisenberg's Uncertainty Principle, you can't observe or measure something without affecting its outcome. While this principle specifically refers to quantum mechanics, it applies almost everywhere. The act of observing something—and especially the attempt to measure it—unintentionally changes what we're measuring. As soon as a church or pastor knows their effectiveness is being evaluated, their behavior changes. It's inevitable. That doesn't mean we shouldn't assess a church's health and effectiveness, but we need to be aware that it has side effects. Attempting to measure the essential aspects of the church changes the way we perceive and relate to them. Seldom for the better.

Could it be that we're unintentionally devaluing the church when we place so much emphasis on trying to measure the immeasurable?

Goldilocks Metrics

There is a tendency to consider all metrics as good metrics, as long as they're accurate. As seen in the next diagram, we have a "more is better" approach, with the value of metrics increasing as we pay more attention to them.

"MORE IS BETTER" APPROACH TO METRICS

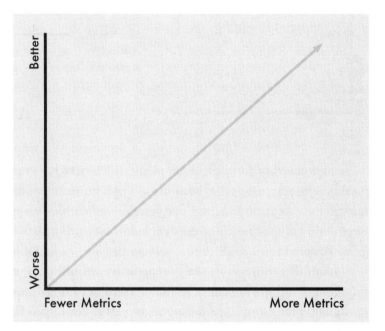

Not only is there not a direct one-to-one correlation between "better" and "more" in regard to metrics, but the amount of attention we should pay to metrics also depends on the size of church we're serving. Simply put, the smaller the church, the less helpful metrics are; the larger the church, the more helpful metrics are. No church should ever ignore metrics, and no church should base everything on them. At either end there is danger. In the middle is a sweet spot, which I call Goldilocks Metrics, where the amount of attention is just right, as seen in the following diagram.

GOLDILOCKS APPROACH TO METRICS-JUST RIGHT

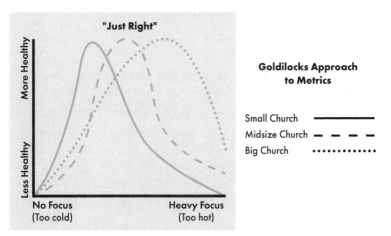

In large churches the emphasis on metrics is heavy, so the sweet spot moves further to the right, because the bigger the numbers, the more relevant the data. In a large congregation, a lack of relevant, objective data is likely to lead to poor decision-making. But metrics are less important in a small church because they are less useful in small groups. The error is more likely to happen when small churches rely *too much* on data instead of relational dynamics and spiritual growth. Not recognizing these differences can often cause stress for small church leaders, since their primary examples come from big churches, and the reports they need to send to their denominational representative are almost entirely metrics-based.

A small church still uses numbers, but it doesn't rely on them as much as large churches do. Instead, they lean heavily on anecdotal evidence. Yes, anecdotes. As they worship and serve together, small churches pay attention to what works and what doesn't through conversations, stories, and personal experience. In a smaller church, if you live closely with people, pay attention to successes and failures, and have enough conversations, you end up with enough anecdotes to become solid evidence.

Megachurch Design Deficits

After retiring from New York City's Redeemer Presbyterian Church, Tim Keller (who went to be with the Lord as I was writing this) wrote a series of tweets outlining eight reasons why leadership separated the church into several congregations after his departure. Keller outlined some of the reasons in Jessica Lea's article, "8 Reasons from Tim Keller Not to Give a Megachurch to a Single Successor":

> "Megachurches have some design deficits," said Keller, explaining his first reason. "In general, they are poor places for formation and pastoral care due to their size. In our current cultural moment that is a deadly problem because Christians are being more formed by social media than local Christian community. We need thick communities and the size of our churches factor into that." [. . .] When megachurches grow quickly under one leader, Keller explained, "they usually depend too much on the gifts and personality of that founder so the sooner that addictive dependence is broken, the better."[9]

Obviously, Keller was not against big churches, but as the founder and longtime pastor of one of the country's most influential megachurches, he was uniquely situated to see their downsides. According to Lea, Keller believed "that having multiple, small congregations is a greater benefit to a city than it would be to have one large church body" and that "cities and regions can benefit from the unique resources of a megachurch (e.g., counseling centers, seminaries). But in general, the area—and the Christians—will benefit more from 10 churches of 400 scattered throughout the city, rather than one church of 4,000 in the middle of it."[10]

Certainly, there are thousands of small-church pastors who could outline similar downsides in the structure of smaller congregations. And that's the point. No size has all the kinks ironed out. Each has its advantages and disadvantages. We need to lean into the strength of every size, while recognizing and making the proper adjustments for their deficits.

The Cost of Chasing Big

Chasing bigness comes at a cost. Too high a cost. Most of us are aware of the costs when pastors achieve big numbers at the expense of their integrity. But the cost is just as steep in the lives of pastors whose churches don't get bigger, no matter how hard they chase it. As one small-church pastor wrote, reflecting feelings that have been felt by countless others, "If church attendance was up, I was up; if it was down, so was I. And the numbers had been going down for a long time."[11]

Something happens to a lot of us shortly after getting into pastoral ministry. We get wrapped in the numbers game very quickly. One of the reasons for this dangerous shift in emphasis is that we're told that any church demonstrating healthy qualities will inevitably become bigger. Then, when the expected numerical growth doesn't occur, we think something is wrong, so we push to get the numbers up. When church attendance numbers go up as a natural result of health, Christ is honored, and the church (local and global) gets stronger. But when church attendance numbers go up because we're using artificial means there are . . .

So. Many. Bad. Outcomes.

Chapter 11

Size, Scale, and Influence

*Though many small churches are
struggling to reach their changing communities,
other small churches are doing an amazing
job of impacting people for Christ in spite of
limited resources and manpower.*

Terry W. Dorsett

In any small town or neighborhood there are a dozen to twenty
people who have an outsized influence. I'm not referring to people
with a title, like the mayor or the owner of the largest business in
town. I'm referring to average people with the gift of influence. The
stay-at-home mom who opens her home to the neighborhood kids,
the delivery driver everyone knows, the retiree neighbors go to for
advice.

Now imagine that this dozen to twenty people with outsized
positive influence (let's call them the 12–20) discover each other and
decide to meet once a week to figure out how they can be an even
bigger influence by pooling their resources, strategizing, and learning from each other. By doing this, their outsized positive influence

becomes even more effective. Now imagine this once-a-week strategy meeting of the 12–20 is your church service.

Sit with that for a moment.

We usually look at a church of a dozen to twenty people as a failure. But if those people were the 12–20 influencers, it wouldn't matter how big the church was. It's tempting to think, "And what if we increased the numbers from 12–20 to 120–200, or even 1,200–2,000? Wouldn't it be great to multiply our influence?" Of course, it would be great. But that's not how numbers work. A group of 120 people does not have ten times the influence of a group of twelve. It will likely only be two or three times the influence. Influence leverages small numbers for big impact. It doesn't scale for crowds. When the crowd grows, the influence may increase, but the amount of leverage (impact per person) always drops.

This, again, is not to put down big churches or large groups. It's simply a way to acknowledge that intentionally small churches are not a problem to be fixed. If they minister strategically, ten churches of 50 can have a far greater impact than one church of 500.

Church growth proponents are seeing this too. A popular saying in church leadership today is, "Engagement is the new attendance." As best as I can determine, it was popularized (and maybe created) by Carey Nieuwhof.[1] And he's right. For bigger churches, it's much more important, accurate, and helpful to measure the engagement of church members.

But it's less true and therefore less helpful for smaller churches. In smaller congregations, the issue is not more engagement. In most small churches, the people are very engaged in the life of the church (in unhealthy small churches, they may be *too* engaged). So, the smaller the congregation, the more important it becomes to emphasize influence more than attendance or engagement.

The Downside of Scaling Up

In March 1948, Howard "Doc" Pierce, the national poultry research director for A&P Foods, held the first Chicken of Tomorrow contest. If you've ever leafed through grandma's cookbook, you may have seen references to different kinds of chickens, called broilers (as little as 1.5 pounds), roasters (medium), fryers (large), and fowl (old and tough). The smaller chickens were more tender, more flavorful, and (here's the problem Doc Pierce wanted to solve) much more expensive.

Pierce's concern was both monetary and humanitarian. He wondered if there was a way to produce chickens under more consistent conditions, so they'd be bigger and less expensive. It's hard for us to imagine in most of the developed world today, but there was a time when "a chicken in every pot" was a significant promise of prosperity.[2] If Doc Pierce's contest opened the door for more families to eat meat, while also selling more chickens at a higher profit, everybody wins, right? Maybe.

Doc Pierce offered a $10,000 reward (a king's ransom in 1948) to the farmer who could breed a chicken that came closest to his idea of perfect, so he sent wax replicas of idealized large-breasted chickens to farmers all over the US. (No, I'm not making this up. You can check out the entire thoroughly entertaining and enlightening story in *The Dorito Effect* by Mark Schatzker.[3])

The contest was held in 1948 and again in 1949. Chickens were bred in farms and factories, then their eggs (31,680 eggs from twenty-five states) were sent to Maryland. After being hatched, the chickens were all fed the same scientifically balanced feed. When full-grown, they were assessed for everything from size and color to the appearance of their skin. Almost everything was evaluated, except for two aspects: no one tested them for flavor or nutrition. When your goal is raising larger chickens for less money, those aren't a primary concern.

As a result, the average size of chickens increased from 2.2 pounds to over three pounds almost immediately, and the time it took to get there dropped from sixteen weeks to twelve weeks. In the ensuing years, the average sizes have continued to rise, while the average time and cost to become full-grown has kept dropping. Today's chickens average 5.7 pounds and can grow as big as nine pounds[4] in just four weeks.[5] For size, efficiency, cost, and availability, the chicken contest was a win-win. But for taste and nutrition, it's a lose-lose. We're not getting 3.5 pounds more chicken per bird; we're mostly getting more water and other non-nutritional fillers. This is why everything tastes like chicken. Because today's chicken doesn't taste like anything.

What's true of chickens is true of almost all the food we consume now. It's grown, packaged, and served faster and cheaper. But it's also less flavorful and less nutritious. The upside is that we can feed more people than before. But even that substantial benefit doesn't come without a cost.

Bigger isn't always better.

It's no coincidence that Donald McGavran's research into church growth methods has a significant timeline overlap with Doc Pierce's research. McGavran started with the best of intentions, trying to understand how entire people groups come to Jesus. But, unlike Pierce, he also foresaw the potential dangers. And he didn't only warn us about them, he held us back from them for as long as he could. But like bigger, but not necessarily better, chickens, once the code was cracked, the floodgates opened.

When non-organic products scale up, they often get better in both quality and cost. From concept to distribution, modern scaling systems work. Our computers, cars, and shoes keep getting better because companies make millions of them. But beyond a certain natural point, scaling up has an inverse effect on the quality of living organisms. Not only is bigger not better, in many ways bigger makes it worse. This is especially true in relationally based organisms like the church.

There is not a single, essential New Testament aspect of the church that requires scaling up. On the contrary, scaling up a church almost inevitably creates at least as many problems as it solves. That's why healthy churches work hard to maintain a sense of smallness, no matter how big they get. Certainly, as a church gets bigger, they can do the technical things better. They can buy and maintain larger facilities, hire more staff, and so on. But, while those improvements are helpful, none of them are essential to the mission. If the church was a business, our product would be relationships—with God and with each other. Relationships don't scale up. They scale down. They need a smaller environment to flourish, either in a small church, or within small groups in a big church.

Content is scalable. Mentoring and discipleship are not.

Content is scalable. Mentoring and discipleship are not.

It's tempting to think that numerical growth is always good and that we can take anything to scale if we apply the right principles, but most of the essential aspects of faith are not scalable. We need to know the difference between numerical growth that's healthy and numerical growth that's dangerous.

Here are a few hints as to when numerical growth is to be avoided, instead of pursued:

- When it causes you to abandon personal connections
- When it creates less margin in your life
- When it's not what God is calling you to do
- When it's an excuse not to go deeper
- When you're doing it to keep up appearances
- When it's not the best way to do what needs to be done
- When it's artificial

- When it causes you to compromise
- When it can't be maintained for the long haul
- When it reduces quality
- When it feels forced

Better than Scale

Over the years I've asked hundreds of pastors, "When you started in ministry, what did you imagine yourself doing on a daily basis?" Invariably, the answers are along the lines of preaching, sermon prep, studying, visiting the sick, caring for the congregation, reaching the community, and the like. They're almost exclusively small-church pastor duties. It's extremely rare for a pastor to say they imagined themselves managing a large staff, raising funds for new facilities, or other large-scale projects. None of that is wrong, of course. I'm grateful for people who have the calling and gifting to work on large-scale projects, and I've greatly benefited from them. But when scaling up becomes the standard for ministry, we create an environment where the natural ministry calling for most pastors feels inadequate. The question church leaders need to ask is not, "How can we scale this up?" but, "How can we do more effective ministry?" If the answer includes scaling up, then by all means, go 10x or 100x. But we can't start with the assumption that scale equals success because in many (maybe most) cases, it's not true.

Here's another example that shows we're too obsessed with church size. While most pastors can name several megachurches and their pastors (several of which I've mentioned already), it's highly unlikely that we're able to name a current people movement without looking it up. We know they are happening. Movements in which people came to Jesus *en masse* were the basis for Donald McGavran's studies, and they keep popping up in pockets of Africa, Asia, and Latin America. Yet we're familiar with the names of a lot of big churches, but none of the big movements. Some of the reason, I'll acknowledge, is that they're not happening in America, where we'd know about them very quickly (note the instant and huge publicity for the short-lived, student-led revival in Asbury University in February 2023). But it's still noteworthy that we pay so much attention to the numerical growth of congregations, but almost no time studying—as McGavran did—the movements where people are coming to faith in Christ in massive numbers. One of the main hallmarks of these people movements is that they're the result of the multiplication of smaller churches, and they seldom result in big churches.

The Frog Is Jumping Out of the Kettle

In 1990, George Barna wrote *The Frog in the Kettle: What Christians Need to Know About Life in the Year 2000*. This was one of the first popular books to use demographics to grasp what was happening in the American church and what might be coming. The title comes from the often told (but untrue) story that, if you put a frog in a kettle and turn up the heat extremely slowly, the cold-blooded amphibian won't notice the change in temperature until it's been boiled to death. Barna, of course, didn't invent the metaphor. It's a common way of explaining how humans can miss big changes if they happen slowly and systemically.

Because of Barna's insightful book and its catchy title, that metaphor became so overused that it quickly wore out its welcome. But the premise was valid. There were several generations of churchgoers who were very satisfied with church-as-usual, with very little thought as to how the message was being heard, or if it was being heard at all. When pastors and other church leaders gathered and discussed the biggest challenges facing the church at that time, apathy topped the list. "People don't seem to want to get involved," they would say. "They attend, they sit and listen, then they go home and do nothing about it." The frog was sitting passively in the church kettle while the culture around us was heating up.

Not anymore. While there is no shortage of apathetic church attendees, that's not the primary conversation among pastors today. Instead of "Why can't I get church members to pay attention?", it's more likely to be "Where did everyone go?" or "Why is everyone so angry?" Unlike the fable, actual frogs will not sit passively as the heat rises. Neither will people. They've jumped out of the kettle. I say, good for them. Instead of sitting passively in an environment that isn't conducive to their spiritual life and growth, this generation is saying "I'm out of here." No, this isn't an ideal situation. But I would suggest that leaving a place where they aren't truly engaged, where they don't really believe, and where there's no effect on their day-to-day lives isn't any worse than staying and stewing. The church member of yesteryear who wasn't happy with the church would remain, complain, and withhold their tithes. The church member of today who isn't happy leaves. This isn't necessarily a *better* option, but I do think it's more honest. And it's getting our attention.

A headline from March 2021 announced the ominous news, "U.S. Church Membership Falls Below Majority for First Time." According to Gallup, only 47 percent of US adults belonged to a religious organization in 2020. In 1999, it had been 70 percent, while back in 1947 membership was at its highest point of 76 percent.[6] Church membership is way down from those lofty heights.

The Gallup headline grabbed a lot of attention because it confirms the perception that America used to be far more Christian in the past, with almost everyone attending church from the pilgrims through the 1950s. But the news is not as bad as it may seem. To begin with, "first time" in the title of the article means the first time since 1943, when Gallup started keeping records of church membership, not the first time in American history. According to Glenn Stanton, if you look further back, you'll see that America was not always the church-going nation we've pictured. "In 1776, only 17 percent of Americans attended a local church. . . . By 1850, that number mushroomed to 34 percent of Americans, and in 1906, 51 percent attended church."[7]

By 1939 (the first year Gallup started keeping track of attendance, not just membership), church attendance had dipped again to 41 percent.[8] In 2019, it was 45 percent.* So, the idea that church attendance is on a perpetual downward slide is not borne out by the data, as seen in the following graph.

US CHURCH ATTENDANCE

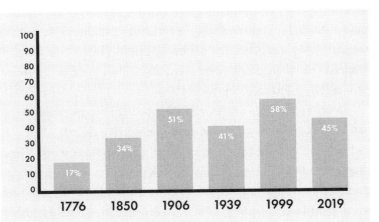

Did you catch that? *Seventeen percent church attendance in 1776!* That makes today's membership and attendance stats far less jarring than we've been led to believe. Author Ed Stetzer agrees, and boldly claims, "No real researcher actually believes Christianity is dying in America."[9] Instead, Stetzer and others make the case that there is a sifting and shifting going on. Church attendees who were only attending out of habit or tradition no longer feel the need to attend

---

*This is the combination of those who attend weekly, monthly, and occasionally. It does not include those who attend seldom. When that is included (which some church statisticians do), the number jumps to 69 percent.

church or check the "Christian" box on surveys. "The nominal Christians are shedding the title, they are becoming secular people without changing their behavior," says Stetzer.

In addition, we need to remember that the American church is not *the* church. Throughout the world, the body of Christ continues to grow at dramatic rates. Nevertheless, the recent declines in Christian attendance and identification are a cause for concern.

What we need to know is whether our obsession with bigness and celebrity has anything to do with the frog jumping out of the church kettle. It would seem so. As reported in Charisma News, a 2023 survey by Barna discovered that while people continue to have relatively high trust in "Jesus (71%), Spirituality (65%), the Bible (63%) and Christianity in general (57%)" and moderate trust in "churches in their community (47%) and Christian pastors or priests (44%)," the bottom dropped out when people were asked about their trust in "celebrity pastors (17%) and megachurches (16%)."

In her memoir, *All My Knotted-Up Life*, Beth Moore recounts the first time she showed up at the small Presbyterian church where she and her husband Keith would eventually become members: "To a couple who'd come of age during the peak years of evangelism's megachurch, the building seemed small. I love the loudness of 3,000-seat worship centers. The energy of it. . . . I loved it. I still love it. But we knew this time around the last thing we were looking for was big."[11] Beth and Keith are not alone. For a whole lot of people, the last thing they're looking for in their faith is big, especially after a season of pain. Even if the church is small, they can sense when it's striving for bigness. People want a church where they won't be seen as an audience member, a giving unit, or a member of a desirable demographic, but as a person who is worthy of the slow, deliberate ministry that can only happen when we stop chasing numbers and de-size the church.

Part 4

HOW TO START
DE-SIZING

Chapter 12

Integrity Is the New Competence

*Growth in size has often
supplanted growth in holiness.*

Katelyn Beaty

So, we've seen where our obsession with bigness came from, and why it's dangerous. But what can be done about it? As we tackle that enormous but essential question in this final segment of the book, we'll start by looking at two overall principles, then we'll outline some practical de-sizing steps that can be taken by pastors, then congregations, and finally by evangelicals as a whole. But before we look at practical steps, we must pay attention to the principles that are foundational to everything we do going forward. We cannot program our way out of the mess we've created. We have to start at the root. First up, restoring our integrity.

* * * *

Three major church waves have appeared in my lifetime: revivalism, strategizing, and activism.

In the revival era of the 1960s and '70s, my father pastored a

Pentecostal church that experienced many legitimate manifestations of spiritual gifts. Meanwhile, in places like New York and California, people like David Wilkerson, Chuck Smith, and John Wimber pastored churches that became touchpoints for entire movements. Then, in the 1980s–90s, I watched as this wave of revivalism slowly waned, with little remaining aside from controversial niche pockets in places like Brownsville, Florida; Toronto, Canada; London, England; and Redding, California.

As revivalism ebbed, strategizing rose. From the 1980s through the 2000s, pastors such as Rick Warren, Bill Hybels, and Andy Stanley led churches that became massive congregations. They wrote books and held conferences to tell thousands of pastors about the strategies they used to create an environment in which massive growth could occur. Leadership became the buzzword as pastors looked to innovators and entrepreneurs, both inside and outside the church, for ways to create a better church culture, lead change, and cast a compelling vision.

Then, in the 2010s and 2020s, activism came in like a rocket on steroids. From the Tea Party and Make America Great Again on the right, to Black Lives Matter and the LGBTQ movement on the left, activists started demanding that their pastor pick a side and fly their (literal) flag or pay the consequences and be canceled.

Certainly, all three of these waves are always present. And, depending on where you live and how old you are, you may have experienced them in very different ways, at different extremes, and in different eras than I did. But if you look back through church history, these three waves—revivalism, strategizing, and activism—are always rising and ebbing among us. It can be very confusing and exhausting, especially when you're unaware of them.

We all have a tendency toward one of these waves. Revivalist pastors pray for an outpouring of spiritual fervor. Strategists (my default) read, study, and experiment with new ideas in search of better ways to do church. Activists want a cause to believe in. But they all have one thing in common: the success of their viewpoint is always confirmed by numbers. The revivalist points to how many people have been attending services and how many days, weeks, months, or years it's been ongoing. The strategist plots everything on spreadsheets to assess, adjust, and confirm their results. The activist wants to recruit everyone to their cause so they can vote in greater numbers than their opposition.

So, what's the answer? Do we need a new revival? Yes. Better strategies? For sure. Passion for important causes? Absolutely. But they all pale when compared to one aspect of life that provides the foundation on which anything of lasting value is built.

Integrity.

Integrity is not a wave. It's not trendy. And it needs no numerical validation. Revivalism cools. Strategies change. Activism burns out. Integrity lasts. But what is integrity?

Simply put, when someone is living with integrity, their everyday behavior matches their highest ideals. No one but Jesus ever lived that way, of course. But when Jesus called us to follow Him, integrity was at the core of that calling.

We see calls to integrity all over the Bible:

- I urge you to live a life worthy of the calling you have received. (Eph. 4:1)
- Follow my example, as I follow the example of Christ. (1 Cor. 11:1)
- Whoever can be trusted with very little can also be trusted with much, and whoever is dishonest with very little will also be dishonest with much. (Luke 16:10)
- If anyone, then, knows the good they ought to do and doesn't do it, it is sin for them. (James 4:17)
- Do not merely listen to the word, and so deceive yourselves. Do what it says. (James 1:22)

It's fascinating that we don't see any such biblical calls for numerical increase. There are more than occasional mentions of numbers and counting, but there's never a call to increase them. We're constantly called to strengthen our integrity. We're never called to increase our numbers.

The base word of integrity is integer. In mathematics, an integer means a whole number. In life, integrity means a whole person. God has called us to be people of integrity for our own good as well as to honor the One in whose image we have been created.

What Leadership Rises and Falls On

John Maxwell (one of the experts in the strategizing wave) is famous for saying, "Everything rises and falls on leadership."[1] It's become popular because it's so obvious and indisputable, right? Maybe, maybe not. Certainly, leadership is important. In the business world, it's indispensable. But according to Jesus, all our ideas about power and leadership are supposed to be upside-down in the kingdom of God. The first shall be last, the last shall be first. A little child shall lead them. The humble will be exalted. I could go on (Jesus did).

But for now, let's roll with the common perception that everything rises and falls on leadership. If so, what does leadership rise and fall on? I would suggest that leadership can rise on many things. It can rise on talent, hard work, charisma, a great idea, a compelling narrative, a job promotion, and more. The question of what leadership rises on is so multifaceted as to be confusing.

But what is leadership maintained by? That's much clearer. In the church it can only be held, especially over the long term, by one thing.

Integrity.

If everything rises and falls on leadership, leadership rests on integrity. And what causes leadership to fall more readily than all other reasons combined?

A lack of integrity.

After all the leadership books have been read, studied, and stacked on your shelf, the only real question anyone is asking from the position of follower is simple: "Can I trust this person?" You may call it integrity, character, moral fiber, or something else (I will use character and integrity interchangeably in this chapter), but it all comes down to one simple thing: do your actions match your ideals? We need to move from an obsession over size and methods to a re-establishment of personal and ecclesiastical integrity.

Where Does Integrity Come From?

The church will never fail due to *our* lack of integrity. It's Jesus' church, and He has more than enough integrity to maintain it from now through eternity. What *is* at stake is our role in His church, the perception of the church by those outside the fold, and the growing list of people who are hurt whenever we fail the integrity test.

If we want to be people of integrity, there's only one way to get there, with four simple, but profound steps:

We need to:
1. Do the right thing
2. Every time
3. For a long time
4. With no agenda

Whenever I teach this, no one ever has a question about steps one through three. It's that fourth one that gets the hands going up. The agenda gets us in trouble.

But isn't the agenda to bring glory to God? Like Jesus taught in the Sermon on the Mount, "Let your light shine before others, that they may see your good deeds and glorify your Father in heaven."[2] Isn't that our agenda?

> **No one who has deconstructed their faith has done so because they saw a deficiency in the technical excellence of church services.**

No, it's not. The glory of God is not our agenda; it's the ultimate anti-agenda. An agenda implies an ulterior motive, something sneaky and underhanded. Doing good simply for the glory of God undermines every agenda.

There is no shortcut. Character doesn't just happen. It only works if you work at it. The more intentionally you practice it, the better you get at it. And the more you neglect it or get relaxed about it, the less well you do it. When phrases like "God wants us to do everything with excellence" or "Go big or go home" become a rallying cry, we're elevating technical prowess above character. We're putting gifts of the Spirit above fruit of the Spirit, and competence above character. When we do that, we open the door for all manner of abuses to become excused, then commonplace, then defended.

Integrity happens when we go small but consistently for a long time.

"Go big or go home" is a lie. It's not motivating. It's guilt-inducing. And debilitating. No one who has deconstructed their faith has done so because they saw a deficiency in the technical excellence of church services. But many have left because of a lack of integrity in the church's leaders or members. We cannot pursue both size and integrity at the same time. We have to choose one over the other. If we truly want to reach a hurting world with the gospel of Jesus for the glory of God, we must be people of integrity.

It may seem like there is plenty of evidence to the contrary. After all, church history is filled with religious leaders in great positions of power who have questionable integrity, even outright deplorable behavior. But in the long run, that's not what engenders long-term trust or creates strong churches. Church members "evaluate the quality of preaching, not by the loftiness of a person's ideas, but by their level of trust in the preacher as a person," Adam McHugh reminds us. "A recent study found that the credibility of a preacher is first a function of the *relationships* they have with their listeners."[3]

Instead of setting bigger goals, set a moral compass. Instead of counting people, be someone who can be counted on. Instead of pushing for goals, live by principles. No amount of skill, money, or up-and-to-the-right numbers on a church attendance graph can compensate for a flawed character. Or, to put it more poetically as David Brooks did, "You can't compensate for having a foundation made of quicksand by building a new story on top."[4]

We need a revival of integrity. We need to study integrity at least as hard as we've been studying strategy, pursuing activism, and desiring revival. We need to actively pursue personal and mutual integrity, not just as a character trait, but as a learned skill. Then sharpen that skill like our lives and reputations depended on it. Because they do.

The Bigness-Integrity Gap

Look at the following lists of words. In the first list are some of the words we use when we're pursuing bigness, while the second one shows some of the character traits of integrity.

BIGNESS VS. INTEGRITY

BIGNESS
Efficiency, Leadership, Success, Hustle, Increase, Growth, Excitement, Effectiveness, Passion

INTEGRITY
Love, Joy, Peace, Patience, Kindness, Goodness, Faithfulness, Gentleness, Self-control

The first thing to note is that there's nothing inherently wrong with anything in the first list. I have used every one of them on a regular basis, with no apologies. Indeed, many times these traits were necessary ingredients in accomplishing difficult tasks. We rightly admire people with the skills of leadership, hustle, and passion. But it's possible to become highly adept at all of them, yet still lack integrity. You don't need to be a person of character to be efficient, successful, or passionate. Now, many will argue that the traits in the first list are made better by those in the second list, and I would agree wholeheartedly. Not only is a leader of strong character far better for the long-term prospects of any business or project, the opposite is also true. Using those skills without the undergirding of character is a house of sand that will eventually collapse. Adding the Integrity list to the Bigness list is always better in the long run.

The second list works entirely differently, though. First, if it looks familiar, it's because it's from the fruit of the Spirit in Galatians 5:22–23. There are so many additional positive character traits in the Bible (wisdom, justice, generosity, and so on), but this is the ultimate starter list.

Second, note the contrast between the lists. While the traits in the first list can be seen as "not necessarily bad," the traits in the second list are essential for people of character. I can live without a person of passion and efficiency in my life, but I cannot—will not— spend any more than the minimum required amount of time with people who are missing any of items on the character list. Loving, but not patient? No. Gentle, but lacking in self-control? Not a chance. In fact, I would argue that those character traits are so intertwined that you can't exhibit any without having them all. It's impossible to be truly kind but not faithful, or joyous but not at peace.

Third, there will be times when the demands of the one list will conflict with the other. In certain situations, our desire to hustle will challenge our need to be patient, and our passion will fight against our self-control. When the lists come in conflict, which they do on a regular basis, the person who is pursuing character must always—absolutely *always*—choose to follow character instead of bigness.

As always, Jesus said it best: no one can serve two masters because that's when we experience a loss of integrity. Of course, I'm referring to Jesus' teaching on mammon, a passage we tend to speak about only when referring to money. But mammon means much more than that. So, let's take a moment for a quick lesson in biblical languages.

The New Testament was written in Greek, the Old Testament in Hebrew. But there is a smattering of Aramaic in the New Testament and in the later books of the Old Testament. This is because they were written during or shortly after the era when the Assyrians were a world power, and their language became commonplace. In the first century, the everyday spoken language of most Jews, including Jesus and the disciples, was Aramaic. For instance, when Jesus was on the cross, He quoted from Psalm 22:1, but He did so in the Aramaic language, saying *"Eloi, Eloi, lama sabachthani?"* which means "My God, my God, why have you forsaken me?" But, if everything else Jesus said is translated into Greek in the gospels, why did Mark and Matthew quote Him in Aramaic in this instance? Because *Eloi* in Aramaic was misunderstood as a call to Elijah by the Latin-speaking Romans, rather than the cry to God that it was. The Aramaic held a place in the story that the Greek translation alone could not tell us.

Likewise, in Jesus' teaching about mammon, I think the newer translators who use "money" here instead of the Aramaic word *mammon* make a mistake. Mammon can mean money, of course. And in this passage, money was the subject at hand. But if money was all Jesus meant, why didn't the original authors use one of the Greek terms for money, instead of keeping one Aramaic term in the middle of an otherwise Greek passage?[5] Because mammon is more than a neutral term for money. It means, or at least strongly implies, an unhealthy hunger for riches, much like the term "filthy lucre" did for generations, or like "all about the Benjamins" might mean today. Whatever mammon might technically stand for, in both instances when Jesus used the term (Luke 16:9–13; Matt. 6:24), He was talking about a divided heart. One that was not integrated but split into divided loyalties. In this context, Jesus' use of the term mammon can mean something other than money. Mammon is anything that tugs our hearts to such a degree that it might replace the spot only God should occupy. In both instances of the term, Jesus is not describing money in morally neutral terms, but as a stand-in for the desire for more. Our desire for mammon could be the drive for more money, or power, or fame. In many churches, pastors have spent too much time trying to explain why mammon/money *doesn't* mean you can't get rich, but we sometimes fail to describe what it *does* mean.

Mammon = the drive for more.[6] More money, more power, more platform.

We cannot serve God properly while constantly driving to the hoop for more. This was Jesus' primary point. Those two drives—the drive to serve Jesus and the drive for more—will come into conflict, not once but constantly. If we want Jesus *and more* of anything, we will serve the one (bigger numbers) and not the other (God). We need to make up our minds that our goal is not Jesus *and* a bigger congregation, just Jesus, no matter the size of the congregation. We cannot serve God and numbers.

Cognitive Dissonance

Every time we say yes to the numbers, we divide our loyalties. Then it becomes easier to divide them the next time, and the next. Before long we're living permanently in a state of dis-integrity, causing so many of us to come apart (dis-integrate) long before we've completed the call that God gave us. Psychologists call it cognitive dissonance. It happens when we believe one way while living a different way. Jesus was the only person who never had a moment of cognitive dissonance. He never once was at odds with Himself, His Father, or His mission. His thoughts, actions, and beliefs were always in perfect union.

The rest of us live with varying degrees of dissonance. Our minds (cognition) know what we are supposed to do and who we are supposed to be, but our behavior doesn't always match that. The greater the distance between the two, the more severe the dissonance and the harder it is to live with ourselves and others. Something has to give. Either we will raise our behavior to the level of our beliefs, or we will lower our beliefs to the level of our behavior.

Every time we say yes to the numbers, we divide our loyalties.

This is what the apostle Paul laments in Romans 7. His mind is a willing slave to God's law, but "there is another law" that constantly entangles him. The law of sin and death causes him to cry in constant agony, "That which I don't want to do, I keep doing!" and, "Who will deliver me from this body of sin?" We don't know what sins Paul was struggling with. I believe he intentionally left us in the dark about those specifics so we wouldn't assign the dissonance he was struggling with to only one sin or state of mind. But we know there was a Christian celebrity culture at work in Corinth, where he was living when he wrote Romans, because Paul addressed it in 1 Corinthians 1. It doesn't stretch credulity to imagine that the sin Paul might have been fighting in his "inward man" in Romans 7 was the tug toward greater fame, a higher church-plant count, or a larger "I follow Paul" group. Do I really think that is what Paul's Romans 7 struggle was about? Doubtful. But it could have been. The apostle Paul had more reason than anyone outside the Twelve to claim Christian celebrity status, but he wholeheartedly rejected it in the strongest possible terms. As Ryan Lokkesmoe reminds us, "If there was anyone in the first century who would have seemed truly irreplaceable to his team, it was Paul. But Paul didn't view himself that way."[7]

Dissonance doesn't only impact pastors, it affects churchgoers too. First, we start following church leaders who have risen into leadership through their exceptional communication skills, leadership gifts, or because they've positioned themselves as champions for our side of a cultural issue. Then, when a church leader loses their own Romans 7 fight, many rally to their side, not in biblical restoration, but in excuse-making, victim-blaming, and a race to re-platform them because of their exceptional ability to draw a crowd, raise funds, or rally the troops. We ignore, excuse, or applaud sins that we should be denouncing. Cognitive dissonance, meet groupthink—a lethal combination.

Character doesn't come easily. It requires that we walk humbly, not arrogantly; that we serve when we want to lead; that we choose the obscure path, not the spotlight. Most of us want to get to happiness too quickly. We look for a shortcut around the very situations that are necessary to test and strengthen our integrity. No one should want to suffer, of course. That's a mental and emotional problem of its own. But when we do face difficult times, the Bible tells us, "We know that suffering produces perseverance; perseverance, character; and character, hope" (Rom. 5:3–4). The path to character often journeys through fields of pain.

Instead of size, tradition, or style, integrity should be our unifying thread. A traditional church and a cutting-edge church that are led by people of integrity have far more in common than two cutting-edge or two traditional churches in which one has a leader with integrity and the other has a pastor cutting moral and ethical corners.

The Road to Vegas

Throughout this book I've recounted some stories of pastors who have cut those corners. A few of them have very public stories, so, without any desire to pile on, I included their names. But whenever the names weren't known or necessary, I left them out. Now I need to mention one more by name. Mine. There was a time when I, Karl Vaters, came very close to not just cutting corners, but slicing them to shreds. This is a very personal episode in my life that illustrates both the power and the fragility of integrity.

I've been in pastoral ministry for over four decades. Aside from a few years as a staff pastor at a larger church, all of it has been in small churches. For the first twenty-five of those years, I was as much in pursuit of numerical growth as any pastor I know. But the churches I served never became big, no matter how many church growth principles I implemented. After chasing those numbers to no avail, I faced my own stereotypical pastoral burnout, which was recounted in *The Grasshopper Myth*, so I won't retell it all here. But there was one part that I've never written about, and I've only shared in public a handful of times. It was too raw and too painful. But now is the time.

I was burnt out. I had chased bigness for over twenty years with almost no results. Finally, the numbers started to rise. Slowly, then very quickly. I was finally on my way! Or so I thought. Then, even faster than they had gone up, they came crashing down. I had done everything the Church Growth books had told me, but just as the results started to materialize, they were snatched away again. I was reeling. I knew I needed a break, so I told the church leadership that I was taking forty days off. My plan had been to spend the first week in the desert. Yes, the literal desert. Since I was in a desert of the soul, it felt poetic to go to an actual desert, as well. After all, Jesus did it and so did many of the early church monastics, known as the Desert Fathers.

Joshua Tree National Monument (a desert so surreally fascinating that U2 named their most famous album after it) is just over a hundred miles away from where I live. A friend owned a small mobile home on the edge of it, which he agreed to let me use. Then, just before I was set to go, a water pipe in the mobile home burst. The following week was also unavailable, but he assured me that week three was mine. One after another, each week fell apart, until, with only one week left in my forty days, the space was finally ready for me.

While waiting, I had done some helpful and important work, renewing my relationship with Shelley, spending time with family and friends, visiting churches where I could worship with no responsibilities, and seeing a Christian counselor. By the time the desert was finally ready for me, I felt like I was ready for the desert. I wasn't fully healed, but I was a lot stronger than I had been. So, I kissed my wife, got in the car, and started driving east from our Orange County home. I had driven that desert highway many times with family and friends, but never alone. After about an hour on the road, I remembered two important facts: 1) when Jesus went to the desert, the devil was there to tempt Him, and 2) the road to Joshua Tree is also the road to Las Vegas.

Sitting alone in my car, feeling very vulnerable spiritually, mentally, and emotionally, I watched as billboard after billboard flew by, advertising every sin that the aptly named "Sin City" had to offer. Gambling, pornography, gluttony, drunkenness, prostitution—all of it was yelling at me from bright, shiny, two-story-tall billboards.

For over a month I'd been frustrated that I hadn't been able to go to the desert when I had wanted to. It had eaten at me, and for a week or two, it made me even angrier at God than I had been. Now, as I watched the billboards get bigger and the temptations get deeper, I noticed two things about myself. First, I had no desire for any of it. The Lord was restoring my soul, and those temptations had no appeal to me. Second, if I had taken that drive when I'd wanted to a month before, I would not have had the strength to resist their pull. I had grown frustrated every time my friend's place in the desert was unavailable, but it was God protecting me from my worst self. I don't know which sin I'd have succumbed to, but I know that in my previously broken state I would have taken an off-ramp for at least one of them.

It's unimaginable to me how different my life would be today if the Lord had allowed my timing to happen instead of His. I don't know why He protected me from that when others seem to face challenges far greater than I did, but I don't think there's been a month go by since then that I haven't paused to be consciously grateful for God's protection over me when I didn't even know He was doing it.

Here are nine lessons about integrity that I learned in the desert that week:

1. Integrity is hard-won, but it's worth it.

In life and in ministry, integrity is the pearl of great price. It will cost you a lot. But it's worth selling everything else to obtain it. Keeping your integrity may cost you everything you have, but not keeping it will cost you more.

2. Integrity is easily lost.

You can spend a lifetime building your integrity, day by day, brick by brick, but it can disappear in a moment, with one bad decision. That road to Vegas has trapped many people before and since me, including at least one famous pastor/evangelist several decades ago.

3. There are times when our integrity is more vulnerable.

Integrity is a paradox. It is one of the most powerful, yet vulnerable character traits. When it's strong it's virtually impenetrable. But when we're tired, frustrated, frightened, or burnt out, the line between right and wrong becomes threadbare, brittle, and far too easy to break.

4. Our integrity will be tested.

Be sure of it. You can go years, even decades, without feeling any strong temptation to compromise, until a glance, a sound, an aroma, or a face from the past can push you right to the edge.

5. When we're tested, there is a way out.

This is a promise direct from Scripture. No temptation has come to any of us that is not common to humanity. And with that temptation, the Lord always—absolutely *always*—allows a way of escape so we can bear it.[8] We may not always *take* the escape. We may not even appreciate it as the escape that it is. But it's always there.

6. There are lines that, if crossed, make recovery a lot harder.

Before I drove to the desert, I had called an emergency number at a counseling center that my denomination provides for pastors. As I related in *The Grasshopper Myth,* when I called that line, the counselor read off a list of sins and betrayals, asking if I'd committed any of them. When I answered honestly that I hadn't, he told me I was the only pastor in the fourteen years he'd been answering that phone who called him before being caught doing one of them. Because of that, he told me, while my recovery would not be painless, it would be comparatively short. If the road to Vegas had been taken a few weeks earlier, that call would have been very different. As would my life, family, and ministry from that day forward.

7. Get help before it's too late.

It's never too late for God to forgive. But after we cross some lines, it can become too late for certain aspects of our life, ministry, and relationships to be restored. As I learned from the counselor on the pastoral help line, most of us don't reach out for help until we've been caught. Don't wait that long. If you are anywhere close to where I was, I beg you to reach out for help. You can't do this alone.

8. Don't excuse, belittle, or blame your lack of integrity on anyone else.

Your sin is not your spouse's fault. Or God's. Or your parents'. Or cultural decay. Our sin is on us. Only when you own that can you truly repent, find forgiveness, and move forward. If someone who was hurt by your lack of integrity can't accept you back into their lives again, they have that right. Sometimes, they have a moral obligation for their own emotional health to do so. Victim-blaming is a sign that we haven't truly owned up to the reality of the damage we've caused.

9. When we pass the integrity test, we get stronger.

This is such good news. Not only will you never face a temptation that others before you haven't faced, but when you hold firm to the Lord and your convictions, you come out stronger for it.

My week in the desert was not easy. The entire time I was vulnerable, alone, and acutely aware of how close I'd come to ruining a life that I live in constant gratefulness for. But the lessons from that season were deep, real, and lasting. It broke me of my need to seek rewards, to strive for unbiblical goals, and to compare myself with others. Sure, those feelings still rise up on occasion, but instead of being a demand I feel compelled to answer, they're like that buzz you occasionally feel from a phone that's not in your pocket anymore.

Chapter 13

Discipleship Fixes Everything

All numerical markers—increased attendance,
bigger and better programs, a larger budget—
must take a backseat to listening to Jesus.
Jesus calls us to abide and abound in him.

PETER SCAZZERO

W hen I teach at church leadership conferences, I often hold a
Q&A session. At the start of one session several years ago, I
was asked a simple, direct question: "How do I fix Sunday school?"

I responded, "Before I answer that, what is the purpose of Sunday
school?"

The questioner's answer was equally simple and straightforward:
"To help the next generation of Christians love Jesus and know the
Bible."

"That's a great answer," I said. "So, instead of asking how to fix
Sunday school, let's ask, *What's the best way to help the next generation
of Christians love Jesus and know the Bible?* If fixing Sunday school
does that, then fix it. But if something else does that better, do the
other thing instead. We have to stop asking how to fix our structures
and get back to why they exist in the first place."

> **If you have a problem in a church, discipleship is the remedy for it.**

It's the same for the pursuit of numerical growth in our churches. When we ask, "How can we get more people in the building?" we're asking the wrong question. Instead, start with a question that exposes our motives, like "why do we want more people in the church building?" A full building and a massive online presence are not the goals. Making disciples is the goal. So that should be our first and only question. What's the best way to make disciples?

* * * * *

In *Small Church Essentials*, I wrote that "bigger fixes nothing."[1] If you take a small, unhealthy church and make it big, you now have a big, unhealthy church. And that's not better, that's worse. In the years since then, that axiom has proven to be truer than I realized. The fact that something is big or growing doesn't indicate it's good. We need a lot more information than numerical growth to make that determination.

Thankfully, there's a truth on the flip side of "bigger fixes nothing."

Discipleship fixes everything. If you have a problem in a church, discipleship is the remedy for it.

- Divisiveness in the church? Discipleship fixes it.
- Immorality? Discipleship fixes it.
- Lack of leadership? Discipleship fixes it.
- Immaturity? Discipleship fixes it.
- Inadequate finances? Discipleship fixes it.
- Bad theology? Discipleship fixes it.

• Apathy? Discipleship fixes it.
• Ineffectiveness? Discipleship fixes it.

To frame it positively, if there are biblical goals you want to reach, discipleship will get you there.

• Want a healthier church? Make disciples.
• More people coming to Christ? Make disciples.
• Financial stability? Make disciples.
• Raise leaders? Make disciples.
• Deeper worship? Make disciples.
• Greater community impact? Make disciples.
• Help the hurting? Make disciples.
• Unity? Make disciples.

. . . Fixes Everything but This

The one thing discipleship is not guaranteed to fix is a church's size. First, because size (or lack of it) isn't a problem that needs fixing. But also because getting bigger doesn't require discipleship. Plenty of churches have grown numerically without discipleship. In fact, discipleship will often undermine extrabiblical growth engines, such as a charismatic leader or a spectacular stage presentation.

The principles for attracting a crowd are not the same as the principles for changing a life. Ask a typical, numerically growing church for evidence that they're discipling people, and they'll point to their growing numbers. Not just attendance numbers, engagement numbers too. But always numbers. No doubt they'll have some wonderful stories of life transformation as well, but that's not the primary evidence that's usually cited.

This may be the biggest mistake the church has made in the last five decades. Pursuing numbers has been seen as an essential aspect of discipleship. But it's not. Sometimes it's the greatest hindrance to discipleship. Bigness can divert so much of our limited attention and energy away from discipleship that it quickly becomes a replacement for discipleship. Discipleship is the means and the end of what Jesus called us to do. But when we're obsessed with bigness, we see everything as a strategy for numerical growth. Discipleship is not a church growth strategy. Neither are prayer, fellowship, worship, or ministry. Even evangelism is not a church growth strategy. Whenever we see any of Christ's commands and blessings as a strategic move, we're no longer serving Jesus as much as we're serving the endgame of growth.

> **Jesus calls us to be disciples, not church growth strategists. He wants worshipers, not performers. Servants, not celebrities.**

Jesus calls us to be disciples, not church growth strategists. He wants worshipers, not performers. Servants, not celebrities. We can't do both. As Chris Galanos wisely noted, "The late-20th-century church model, in so many applications, requires so much energy and attention that little to nothing is left for anything else, including discipleship."[2]

The Power of Four

In *The Great Evangelical Recession*, John S. Dickerson noted that "academics and sociologists argue over exactly how to measure the success or failure of the evangelical church. But by one scriptural gauge, measuring our success or failure is embarrassingly simple. . . . Are we making disciples?"[3]

In a fascinating podcast conversation, Skye Jethani talked with Barna's David Kinnaman about one possible way to measure discipleship. Here's a small segment:

David Kinnaman: You get what you measure. If the most important indicators of success are how large the church is, that's what we'll look at. [How] do we acknowledge leaders who are actually doing something new and different where it may not look like the biggest church but it's actually the deepest church?

Skye Jethani: The more regularly a person engages with Scripture, the more they tend to grow in their faith, well, that's something we can measure, right? We can put out a survey in our congregation and ask people, maybe anonymously, "how many times a week do you open the Bible and read it?"

David Kinnaman: A lot of data is pointing to this, that the more people are engaged in Scripture and in community, the more discipleship that happens, the more outreach-oriented they are.[4]

So, there are ways to measure spiritual maturity. But it has nothing to do with the size of the church the person may be attending. As it turns out, the main way to determine a person's likely spiritual maturity is how often they engage with the Bible on their own each week.

According to a thorough study conducted by Arnold Cole and Pamela Caudill Ovwigho of the Center for Bible Engagement, behavioral differences exist between Christians who read (or listen to) the Bible at least four days a week and those who do so less often. They write: "These differences include both moral behavior as well as how prepared the individual is to serve God and impact the world."[5]

They discovered that there is nominal spiritual growth for people who read the Bible once, twice, or three times a week. For some behaviors "there is no statistical difference between Christians who read or listen to the Bible two to three days a week and those who do not engage scripture at all or only once a week." But at four days a week, there's an extraordinary statistical jump. According to their research, if you read the Bible on more days than you don't read the Bible, your chances for mature Christian behavior go way up. This difference is so big, they call it "the Power of Four."

This research is thorough, but not exhaustive. No doubt, others will come along and give us a greater understanding of these phenomena, but for now we know this: helping people read or listen to the Bible more often may be the best first step in discipling people toward maturity in Christ. While the statistical anomaly of four times a week may be surprising, the principles behind it should not be. The Bible reassures us often about the importance of reading or hearing God's Word.

- I have hidden your word in my heart that I might not sin against you. (Ps. 119:11)

- Until I (Paul) come, devote yourself to the public reading of Scripture, to exhortation, to teaching. (1 Tim. 4:13 ESV)

- All Scripture is God-breathed and is useful for teaching, rebuking, correcting and training in righteousness, so that the servant of God may be thoroughly equipped for every good work. (2 Tim. 3:16–17)

As Jethani mentioned, this is measurable. I recommend this simple process:

Step 1) Ask congregation members to fill out a one-question survey about how many times they read the Bible in a typical week. Collect the information anonymously and collate the data.

QUESTION BOX: WEEKLY BIBLE READING

How many days do you read the Bible in a typical week?

☐ None   ☐ One   ☐ Two   ☐ Three

☐ Four   ☐ Five   ☐ Six   ☐ Seven

Step 2) Present the results to the church.

Step 3) Teach about the Power of Four, encouraging church members the value of increasing their Bible reading to at least four times a week.

Step 4) Start a Read-Through-the-Bible plan together, teaching from the weekly passages. There's great power and great fun in doing this together.

Step 5) In six months to a year, have everyone retake the survey to see how their Bible engagement has increased.

Step 6) Do it again.

Obviously, reading the Bible is not a cure-all. We all know of cranky Christians who know the Bible inside-out, but who demonstrate almost no spiritual maturity. And discipleship is far more multi-layered than reading the Bible a minimum number of days. Discipleship doesn't end with reading the Bible, but if we can help our congregation read their Bibles at least four times a week, it will be a massive step in the right direction.

Discipleship vs. the Sesame Street Church

We have a passive, consumer-oriented approach to church. So many of our creative ideas for reaching people fall prey to something I call Sesame Street Church. Before the long-running children's show

Sesame Street aired, kids' TV was either slow and boring or pie-in-the-face nonsense. *Sesame Street* made learning fun. Soon, teachers either got mad at *Sesame Street*, or tried to play catch-up and make their classrooms fun. But *Sesame Street* was not the revolution in learning that we thought it was. It was still TV. It moved faster, but it didn't help kids move at all. It still required them to sit and watch passively.

In the 1980s and 90s, churches started moving away from hymns and choirs, and started bringing in drums, guitars, worship teams, and new songs. All of which I love. Like *Sesame Street* before it, these new worship styles had some success. Almost all numerically growing churches today are turning up the rhythm and volume, including the church I serve. Sesame Street Church is better than a boring talking head, but it's not enough. It's not the radical shift that will change the hearts and minds of new generations.

Instead of merely turning up the volume and sound, give them an experiential, hands-on, real-world approach. Offer relational mentoring with a mature believer, create ministry teams that meet community needs, and enforce all of that with teaching and preaching that challenges them to embrace an outside-the-church-walls, Monday-through-Saturday faith. Embracing new worship styles is good, but it's still a mostly passive, audience-oriented process. What new generations want—and all of us need—is a churchgoing experience that starts with worship, prayer, and sermons, but is aimed at getting us out into a world of experienced faith. The new metrics of the church need to start and end with real-world discipleship. And discipleship starts with engagement in God's Word.

Jesus didn't say "go build my church." He said, "I will build my church." For 2,000 years and counting, He's been doing His part. Discipleship is our part.

Chapter 14

De-sizing the Pastor

*Perhaps, the abundant life we've been
seeking has little to do with big events and comes
in a subtler form: embracing the pauses
in between major beats.*

JEFF GOINS

No one is affected more directly by an obsession with church size than the faithful pastors who have been called to serve God's people. We face constant pressure to get our numbers up from denominational leaders, church members, church leadership gurus, and the loudest voice of all, our own heads and hearts telling us we're not enough until we hit that next numerical goal . . . and the next . . . and the next . . .

"We are losing too many pastors," writes Bo Lane in *Why Pastors Quit.* "They are overworked, underpaid, and unprepared."[1] The percentage of pastors wanting to quit ministry has had a significant uptick in recent years, especially in the immediate aftermath of COVID-19 lockdowns. According to Barna, as many as 38 percent of US pastors seriously considered leaving ministry in 2021.[2] But the news is not all bad. According to Gary L. McIntosh, "Such reports are overstated, and controlled studies (versus rumor) point out that turnover among pastors is about the same as for other stressful jobs."[3]

So the news is not as bad as we may have heard, but pastoral ministry should be better than that, shouldn't it? We're supposed to be in the peace-making, stress-relieving business, not sitting in the same stress boat as others. Jesus promised us that His load would be easy and His burden light, not no worse than "other stressful jobs." We need to de-size pastoral ministry.

De-sizing is like losing weight. It doesn't happen easily or automatically; it's filled with forward and backward steps, and it involves the breaking of long-held unhealthy habits. But it can be done. In this chapter, we'll tackle how pastors can de-size and de-stress. In chapter 15 we'll see how to move our congregations toward de-sizing, and then in chapter 16, we'll look at how evangelicalism can start to de-size as well.

How to Know If You Need to De-size

Many pastors are working very hard to push back against the relentless drive for bigness. They're doing great ministry, meeting needs, and honoring Christ in a way that makes sense at their current size. They set non-numerical goals, have a drive to do better every week, and are discipling their members without obsessing over numbers. But even for those pastors, bigness has a subtle, relentless tendency to worm its way in. Here's a short survey to help you know if you have some de-sizing work to do. Be honest. It won't work otherwise. And no one else needs to know. (Although they probably already do.)

DO I NEED TO DE-SIZE?

Circle one response per question

1. When you describe how well/poorly your church is doing, do you tend to use numbers?
Always 5   Usually 4   Often 3   Sometimes 2   Seldom 1   Never 0

---

2. Is your mood or behavior significantly affected by your church's attendance numbers?

Always 5   Usually 4   Often 3   Sometimes 2   Seldom 1   Never 0

3. Do you ever exaggerate your church's attendance figures?

Always 5   Usually 4   Often 3   Sometimes 2   Seldom 1   Never 0

4. Do you ever interpret a drive for bigger numbers as an expression of greater faith?

Always 5   Usually 4   Often 3   Sometimes 2   Seldom 1   Never 0

5. Do you ever feel like your church or ministry is less valuable than someone else's because yours is smaller? Or that a church is better because it's bigger?

Always 5   Usually 4   Often 3   Sometimes 2   Seldom 1   Never 0

6. Do you feel personal pride when your church numbers increase, or shame when they decrease?

Always 5   Usually 4   Often 3   Sometimes 2   Seldom 1   Never 0

7. Do you believe pastors of larger churches are more qualified to teach you about ministry than those who serve in smaller churches?

Always 5   Usually 4   Often 3   Sometimes 2   Seldom 1   Never 0

8. Have you ever overlooked someone's questionable moral behavior (possibly your own) because of numerical results?

Always 5   Usually 4   Often 3   Sometimes 2   Seldom 1   Never 0

9. Do you assume a church must be stuck or broken if attendance isn't increasing?

Always 5   Usually 4   Often 3   Sometimes 2   Seldom 1   Never 0

10. Can you describe what a healthy church looks like without using numbers?

Always 5   Usually 4   Often 3   Sometimes 2   Seldom 1   Never 0

Your Total_____

So, how'd you do?

- 0–15: Congratulations! You've de-sized!
- 16–35: Not bad, but you have some work to do. If this result is higher than expected, you may have thought size wasn't an issue for you, but it's burrowed in a little deeper than you realized.
- 36–50: You have a lot of work to do.

The higher your score, the more obsessed you are with size, and the more de-sizing you'll need to do. The good news is, since you cared enough to take the survey, you can make the necessary changes. Here are some ways to start . . .

Recognize the Value of Inefficiency (Yes, Inefficiency)

We have an unhealthy relationship with time. I like working efficiently. Every time I figure out a new way to work smarter, not harder, it's like finding a $20 bill in an old coat. Efficiency is not just a matter of good work habits, it's about biblical stewardship. But it doesn't work that way in worship.

A great time of worship is like a great work of art or a great relationship. Art, beauty, and love are not efficient. Neither are worship, prayer, or fellowship. They take too much time, and they're too important to rush. This is not an excuse for laziness, apathy, or lack of planning. A wise church leader knows when to use time efficiently and when to spend it generously. Efficient planning should create extravagant expanses of time for the things that can't be rushed.

- Time to worship, not just get through the song set
- Time to pray, not just say a prayer
- Time to fellowship, not just do a turn-and-shake
- Time to disciple people, not just complete the curriculum
- Time to relax instead of worrying about the clock

Efficiency is great, but it's not the only valid way to perceive our usage of time. Much of life, parenting, marriage, friendship, and pastoring requires vast amounts of inefficient time usage. If that sentence made you cringe, I get it. It made me cringe to write it. Yet I stand by it. Most of the important things in life cannot be done with modern methods of time-saving efficiency. They often require slow, ponderous, sometimes boring stretches when nothing seems to be happening. That's often when the most important stuff occurs. We need to do the administrative parts more efficiently so we can slow down for God and people. You know, the *ministry* parts of ministry—loving Jesus, loving each other, and making disciples. You can't hurry that. And why would you want to?

Reconsider the Pastor-as-CEO Model

According to Glenn Packiam, with help from research done by Andrew Root, pastoral authority has been perceived to come from three different sources in three different ages of church history. I have taken Packiam and Root's ideas and labelled them Pastor as Wizard, Pastor as Scholar, and Pastor as CEO.

First, the Pastor as Wizard. In the medieval era, praying for the sick, reading and interpreting the Scriptures, and turning bread/wine into body/blood were seen as nearly magical. In that era, according to Packiam and Root, "the pastor—the *priest*—was anointed with special powers" in the minds of the people. Later, with the rise of the Reformation, the Pastor as Scholar era took hold. "As reformations led to rationalism, the pastor in the post-Enlightenment West found authority in his learning. . . . This began a long tradition of education as the basis for credibility." Today we're solidly in the third era, the Pastor as CEO, which started in the late twentieth century, in which "the authority of a pastor began to come from the institutions they created. . . . With long sermons as a detriment and seminary education as a potential liability, pastors began seeking other ways of establishing their presence in a community. The answer was in building strong and influential churches."[4] The bigger the church, the greater the perceived credibility. Thus, the rise of the megachurch pastor as the ultimate authority.

Packiam correctly notes that none of these were ever the real source of our authority anyway. It was, is, and always will be found not in our perceived magic powers, our education, or the size of our institutions; instead, "the source of our authority is Jesus, and it comes from being in his presence. But that is not all. By being with Jesus, we learn from him what power is *for*."[5] This is what really matters.

In a remarkable moment of honesty and vulnerability, Packiam admits what many pastors often feel. After citing how the church had massive growth for several years, he writes, "I thought this was what I wanted. I mean, a fast-growing church is every pastor's dream. But some lessons are best learned the hard way: turns out, I don't actually *want* to be the CEO/executive director of a nonprofit/HR expert/strategy guru/leader of leaders, etc. I got into this thing to teach the way of Jesus. Is this the way of Jesus?"[6]

The answer is no. The pursuit of bigness and the way of Jesus are not compatible. The God of the Bible has clearly and repeatedly aligned Himself against bigness. He's on the side of the outcast, the forgotten, the abandoned, the under-resourced. He has declared *Himself* the hero of the story, and He will not share His glory with anyone. In Him, the strong do not become stronger, but the weak are made strong. According to the church-planter extraordinaire, the apostle Paul: "God chose the foolish things of the world to shame the wise; God chose the weak things of the world to shame the strong. God chose the lowly things of this world and the despised things— and the things that are not—to nullify the things that are, so that no one may boast before him" (1 Cor. 1:27–29).

Being a high-performing person is exhausting. Whether you fail at it or have success, there will always be another level to achieve.

And someone else will always achieve more. Plus, the very nature of performance creates distance. It requires a stage. It means elevating yourself above others. Distancing yourself from them. This is exactly the opposite of what Christ called His church to be.

Embrace the Pastor-as-Pastor Model

Your church cannot be a great church if the pastor tries to pastor everyone. Or so I keep hearing. But it's not true. Great churches don't happen when we pastor less. And we don't have to pastor more, either. But we need to pastor more biblically. We need to reject the Pastor-as-CEO model, the Pastor-as-Entrepreneur model, the Pastor-as-Celebrity model, and the Pastor-as-Enabler model, and fully embrace the Pastor-as-Pastor model.

The word "pastor" only appears once in most English Bibles (Eph. 4:11–12), alongside apostles, prophets, evangelists, and teachers. (Sometimes translated as "shepherd," which gives us the APEST acronym for the five-fold ministry gifts.) In that passage, the command given to church leaders is not to do the ministry *for* the people, but to "equip God's people for works of service." When church leaders tell us we need to pastor less, they're conflating "pastoring everyone" with "doing everything *for* everyone." But biblical pastors don't *do* everything; biblical pastors *equip* everyone.

When pastors truly embrace their God-ordained role, they will have two responsibilities that come directly from the Ephesians passage: 1) sharing the leadership with the other five-fold ministry gifts, and 2) equipping God's people. This is also one of the best ways to reduce pastoral guilt and exhaustion. Most pastors feel overwhelmed by their limited time. In a recent Q&A session at a pastoral conference, a pastor asked me: "If I spend an hour caring for the people in the church, I feel like I'm stealing an hour from reaching people outside the church. But when I spend an hour reaching people outside the church, I feel like I'm stealing an hour from caring for the people in the church. What should I do?"

The answer is to embrace the Pastor-as-Pastor model. Equip the people in the church to reach the people outside the church.

Stop Playing the Numbers Game

We need to reframe the way we talk about numbers. Instead of saying, "We stayed stuck at 75 last year," or "We grew from 75 to 130 last year!", tell us more of the story, like this: "For the last few years, our church has been stuck. There was inner conflict, and it affected our ability to reach new people for Jesus. But over the last year, the Lord has helped us to resolve our conflicts, renew our commitment to outreach, and become a worshiping, loving congregation! We've grown from 75 unmotivated, angry people to 75 (or 100, or even 65) excited, united people, on mission with Jesus!"

With even the smallest story attached to it, the numbers fade a little as the story takes center stage, as it should. Sure, it takes longer to tell, but it's also more engaging. And even the church with limited, or no numerical increase can highlight what's working instead of feeling guilty over the numbers.

Elevate Stories over Stats

Stories are powerful. They inspire us, inform us, and bring meaning to our lives. Stories are the coat-pegs of the mind, where we hang our ideas, our ideals, and our identities.

When a group has stories in common, they form a bond that is hard to break. The right story can turn enemies into friends, while the wrong story can fracture longstanding alliances into splinters, creating divorces, destroying families and friendships, and causing wars. The stories we tell ourselves can keep a church stuck in an endless cycle of old, unhealthy patterns, or set a new course for a transformative future. When the story we tell with our actions doesn't match the story we tell with our words, that hypocrisy engenders distrust and discord. But when our words and actions tell an integrated story, we can inspire generations.

This is one reason why Jesus always told stories. Both Matthew 13:34 and Mark 4:34 remind us, He did not speak to the crowds without a parable. Jesus knew what all good teachers know. Facts and statistics can support a good narrative, but they can never replace it. Yet that's what we've done in a lot of church leadership over the last couple of generations. We've treated the statistics like they're the story. "We broke all previous church attendance records this weekend!" is a wonderful statistic, but it's not a story. It doesn't become a story until we de-size the statistics and hear about one of those people who came to church and gave their life to Jesus.

One of the many reasons good stories are powerful is because they include an emotional component. They communicate not only what happened, but how a person feels about what happened. Statistics may allow us to draw

We need to regain the power of story, but we can't do that while we stay obsessed with numbers.

conclusions, but they seldom motivate us to make commitments. When we promote stats over story, we've traded down. There's an old poem that starts with the line, "I'd rather see a sermon than hear one any day; I'd rather one should walk with me than merely tell the way."[7] Telling an entertaining story is important, but drawing someone into the story is better. Reinforcing who you are through the stories you tell helps create credibility with the congregation.

One of the main reasons to de-size the church is that for forty-plus years we've abandoned the value of the greatest story ever to chase the lesser components of statistics, demographics, and metadata. We need to regain the power of story, but we can't do that while we stay obsessed with numbers.

Redefine the Competition

Occasionally a pastor will pop up on my social media feed to remind us that our churches are not competing with each other, but that our real competition is people's desire to take a walk in the park, go to the beach on a summer Sunday, or spend a weekend at the lake.

I very much agree with the front half of that sentiment. But the last half is troubling. It presupposes something about the modern church that is consumeristic, passive, and attractional rather than giving, active, and missional. Let's break it down.

First, while I'm grateful to hear that churches should not be in competition with one another, why do we want to reframe ourselves as being in competition with nature walks, beaches, or lakes? God made all those blessings, and they should be enjoyed. The joys of life to be found outside the church walls are not our competition. I'm aware that people will often choose the beach rather than a church service, but viewing beautiful Sunday morning weather as a problem feels tone-deaf at best and near pharisaical at worst.

Second, by framing ourselves that way, we reinforce the idea that church is a thing I go to rather than as the kingdom of God made visible in all the activities of life. It's inaccurate and unhelpful to see the Christian life through the narrow lens of sitting in a room on a Sunday—and especially not with the added image of a kid stuck in a schoolroom, glancing longingly as other kids enjoy a day at the beach. Or, as one popular meme suggests, that sitting on frozen stands in a blizzard watching a football game is behavior worth emulating with our church attendance.

Third, if we frame ourselves as being in competition with a sunny day in the park, we will lose. Thankfully, it's not our competition.

Fourth, Jesus never said anything remotely like this. It's

inconceivable that any New Testament writer would see these bless-ings in competition with the kingdom of God breaking forth upon the earth. The biblical writers clearly identified our enemies, which include the devil,[8] death,[9] and even anxiousness,[10] but even in a world saturated with creation-worshiping paganism, the Bible never pre-sents the beauty of nature in anything but glowing terms as blessings for which we should be grateful.[11]

We need to resist the trap of seeing other churches, a beautiful sunny day, and family time at the park as our competition. This at-titude is the direct result of our numbers-obsessed church culture that prioritizes sitting in the building on Sunday above almost everything else. I'm not naïve. I know there's a growing trend of less frequent attendance, even among faithful churchgoers, and that it has a nega-tive impact on our faith. But blaming that on the joys of a God-given beautiful day is foolhardy and inaccurate. The church is not threat-ened by the beauty in the world God has created.

There's a growing concern that the church is losing the next gen-eration. The good news is that this has been the concern of every generation, yet the church continues to live and thrive. The bad news is we *will* lose the next several generations if we don't stop competing with Hollywood, with the government, with science, or with the beach on a sunny day. Above all, churches must stop competing with each other and start doing the Jesus stuff better. Instead of worrying about putting on a better Sunday morning show, we need to start taking "love one another" more seriously. We need to decide to love God, love others, teach the Word, live our convictions, and do all of it *really well*. If we did that, we'd realize the church truly has no competition.

Chapter 15

De-sizing the Congregation

*We do not find Paul concerning himself with
the size of churches or with questions about
their growth. His primary concern is with their
faithfulness, with the integrity of their witness.*

LESSLIE NEWBIGIN

Recently I was the guest speaker at a conference of church leaders. During lunch as we were talking shop, I asked, "What's been working in your congregations lately?"

"In the last few months, we've had to redefine what kind of church we are," offered one of them.

"Redefine how?" I asked as he paused for a sip of coffee.

"We used to be a church of 140," he said as set his cup on the table. "Since coming back from the lockdowns our average is 90. For a couple of years, we've struggled to get those 50 people back. But I know they aren't coming back. So, I finally admitted that to our leaders and told them we have to stop thinking like the church of 140 we used to be and start thinking like the church of 90 that we are."

He had my attention. "What does that mean for you?" I asked.

"Well, it's meant three important changes, actually. First, it helped us right-size everything, reducing and deleting some ministries, and more accurately allocating our time and resources. Second is the change in our mindset. When we thought of ourselves of a church of 140, an average attendance of 90 felt so deflating. Now it's a normal Sunday. If we had kept seeing ourselves as a church of 140, we could have grown from 90 to 100 and still seen ourselves as down by 40. We could have grown by 50 percent, jumping from 90 to 135, and we'd still be down by 5. But now, if we grow to 100, we're up by 10. And if we're blessed to reach 135, it's 50 percent growth. By accurately defining where we truly are, we're putting ourselves in a better position for health and growth."

"That makes a lot of sense," I responded. "But you said there were three changes. What's the third?"

"Oh, right," he said. "Instead of looking back to some version of the good old days, it's helped us appreciate what we have now. And we're doing great ministry for our size, believing God for many fruitful years to come."

That's one of the healthiest post-pandemic adjustments I've heard any church make. And it's not some mind game that the pastor and church are playing. It's a mind game they've *stopped* playing. They're no longer living in a "we're a church of 140" fantasy; they have an accurate picture of their current reality. This is why de-sizing matters. By accurately assessing and appreciating their current situation, this church is setting themselves up for a future of effective ministry.

De-Sizing Priorities

Life and ministry are a constant battle of priorities. While some of those struggles are between the bad and the good, many of the harder ones are between the good and the not-as-good. Here are several ways local congregations need to constantly assess their priorities:

Model Faithfulness over Performance

When many (maybe most) people reflect on the activities of the church, they think about what happens on the stage. Stages are built for performance. When the performance on the stage takes precedence over the mandate to make disciples, our priorities are backwards. Healthy churches understand that. The focus of a healthy church isn't on the onstage performance, it's on the offstage discipleship.

Value People More than Buildings

There are too many churches that remain unwilling to adapt the facility to the needs of the ministry. This is usually, but not always, led by longtime members who have invested massive amounts of time, money, and emotion into the physical property. I appreciate the sacrifices they made, but healthy churches prioritize people, not buildings. The facilities are a tool to reach people in Jesus' name, not an end in themselves.

Prioritize Generosity over Budgets

Unhealthy churches allow the budget to dictate the ministry. Healthy churches do the opposite. Being generous doesn't mean being reckless with funds; instead, it puts the emphasis where it belongs. Finances, like facilities, are a tool, not a goal. A generous church gives of their money, time, and skills based on the need, not on the budget. Generosity is not about finances; it's gratefulness turned outward.

Put Ministry before Programs

The longer a church exists, the greater the pull to become program-driven instead of ministry-driven. Numbers-obsessed churches tend to be over-programmed. If you ask church members to describe the difference between their ministry and their programs, most will have a hard time making the distinction. So would a lot of pastors. Here's the difference. Ministry is what we do, programs are how we do it. Never let the *how* become more important than the *what*.

Value Truth over Opinions

We all have strong opinions formed by our politics, our culture, our traditions, and so on. But the truth of the gospel message comes first. In unhealthy churches, the loudest opinions win the day. In healthy churches, opinions are respected, but they come a distant second to the truth of the gospel, even if those opinions are held by powerful people, the pastor included.

Prioritize Servanthood over Leadership

"Servant leadership" is a good term. Coined by Robert K. Greenleaf in his 1970 essay "The Servant as Leader,"[1] it has become the go-to way for pastors to describe our approach to ministry. But that term, like "church growth," has unintentionally placed the emphasis on the wrong word. When "servant" is the adjective, "leadership" becomes the focus. But the Bible always makes servanthood the focus. The world seeks great leaders, but as Jesus told us, "It shall not be so among you. But whoever would be great among you must be your servant, and whoever would be first among you must be your slave, even as the Son of Man came not to be served but to serve, and to give his life as a ransom for many" (Matt. 20:26–28 ESV).

De-sized churches don't pursue leaders, hoping they'll adapt to biblical servanthood; they look for servants, some of whom will become leaders. The kingdom of God is about servants who lead, not leaders who serve. That may seem like a semantic difference, but it's not. Shifting the emphasis to servanthood is essential.

See Worship as More than Music

Most churches have an underdeveloped sense of worship. It's seldom considered beyond the twenty minutes or so that we sing together in church. I'm a huge fan of live music. Singers and instrumentalists coming together to fill a room with something greater than the sum of their parts is lifegiving. But worship and music are not the same thing. And music, because it has a very specific, outward-facing skillset, leans toward performance.

Recently, I was in a wonderful church that has no musicians. Not due to theology, they just don't have any musicians right now. But the worship was beautiful, deep, and

> **Healthy, de-sized churches prioritize worship, ministry, discipleship, evangelism, and fellowship not as a means to an end, but as the purpose for which we exist.**

uplifting. I've been in churches with great music and great worship. Sadly, I've also been in churches with great musicianship, but very little worship beneath the performative surface. Healthy churches know the difference.

Prioritize Health over Growth

Numbers-obsessed churches either see health as an engine for numerical increase, or they see numerical increase as confirmation that the church is healthy, even if there's plenty of evidence to the contrary. Healthy, de-sized churches prioritize worship, ministry, discipleship, evangelism, and fellowship not as a means to an end, but as the purpose for which we exist, no matter what size the church is.

Promote What's Effective over What's Big

There are advantages to every size of church. Author and pot-stirrer Malcom Gladwell opined, "There is a set of advantages that have to do with material resources, and there is a set that have to do with the *absence* of material resources—and the reason underdogs win as often as they do is that the latter is sometimes every bit the equal of the former."[2] There are advantages of every size of church, including the so-called underdogs. But you can't see them by comparing a church of 1,000 with a church of 50. The overwhelming numerical gap makes the advantages of the church of 50 almost impossible to see. But if we compare 1,000 people attending one church to 1,000 people attending 20 churches of 50 on average, you have an apples-to-apples comparison. Here are some of the plusses of each situation.

- One church of 1,000 may have well-crafted sermons, but 20 churches of 50 probably have more hands-on pastoring.
- One church of 1,000 probably has higher quality musicianship, but 20 churches of 50 almost always have more people singing along.
- One church of 1,000 may have a great children's ministry facility, but 20 churches of 50 typically have a better student-to-teacher ratio.
- One church of 1,000 will have more paid staff, but 20 churches of 50 will have more volunteers.
- One church of 1,000 probably has a stronger online presence, but 20 churches of 50 may have stronger in-person connections.

And that's just for starters. Different church sizes are needed depending on the kind of ministry God is calling you to. That will change depending on a variety of factors, including the community you're called to serve, the gifts of the pastor, the willingness of the members, the changes in the neighborhood, and much more. And those factors should be constantly monitored and adjusted.

Prioritize Almost Everything over Attendance

On any given Sunday, even the smallest, simplest church service juggles an amazing array of complex issues. But too often we reduce the value of this beautiful, multi-layered gathering of believers, seekers, skeptics, and hypocrites to one overly simplistic metric. Namely, how many people showed up?

Certainly, almost every pastor and church are grateful when church attendance is on the rise, me included. But, if we pay less attention to attendance, what should we pay more attention to? My answer to that is "almost everything." Yes, almost everything else happening in a worship service is more important than how many people are in the room. So here are some alternative questions that are always better to ask than "What was attendance last weekend?"

- Was Jesus the focus of our attention?
- Was the Bible taught well?
- Was hope offered to hurting people?
- Did anyone come to faith in Christ?
- Is there more excitement about the future than longing for the past?
- Are people more prepared to live for Jesus after having been here?
- How is it with your soul?

When we don't pause to remember what really matters, it's too easy for the lure of attendance numbers (both up and down) to become more important than they deserve to be.

Two Helpful Tools to Assess Health Non-numerically

To help with this, I've created two tools to help church leaders assess the health of a congregation non-numerically: the Church Health Assessment Tool and the Healthy Church Log.

The Church Health Assessment Tool

The Church Health Assessment Tool is a survey I created of 16 essential items that anyone can take in about three minutes. The four key categories are simple, and they each include four principles.

1. Theology: Bible, Worship, Salvation, and Discipleship
2. Leadership: Teamwork, Unity, Alignment, and Contextualization
3. Mission: First Impressions, Outreach, Demographics, and Impact
4. Attitude: Creativity, Resilience, Enthusiasm, and Anticipation

You'll find it at karlvaters.com/church-health-assessment. There's also a print version in the Appendix. This survey is not designed to fix problems, but it's a good way to start identifying the strengths and weaknesses of a church without relying on the usual numerical markers (attendance, finances, etc.). As with any survey, the more participants you have, the more accurate your results will be. So, it would be great to encourage everyone in your church to participate. This will also help you understand how different people perceive your congregation. For instance, long-time regular members may consider the church to be friendly and united, but newer folks may not.

The hope is that this survey will give you a quick idea of how well you're doing in the non-numerical aspects of church health, allowing you to celebrate and build on your strengths, while adjusting and correcting your weaknesses. You can take the survey for free with no obligation.

The Healthy Church Log

I introduced a rudimentary model of the Healthy Church Log in *100 Days to a Healthier Church*. Since then, I've developed it as a much more practical tool. The concept is simple. If you're a pastor or church leader, keep track of every event, system, and accomplishment for the next six months, giving each one a grade. Your assessment should not include how many people attended the events, just how well it went compared to what you expected. Even better, choose several people in the church to do this from various ages, backgrounds, and levels of spiritual growth. A group of five or six is ideal.

Then, assess the following:

- Events: This includes church services, Bible studies, board meetings, and more. You can even assess the aspects of your Sunday service, giving separate grades to the worship, the sermon, and so on.

- Systems: These are functions of the church that don't necessarily have events attached to them, including your system for receiving, counting, and tracking finances, how decisions are made, your organizational structures for Sunday set-up and tear-down, keeping track of members, campus security, and so on.

- Accomplishments: So much of what happens in a church is unquantifiable, but it's helpful to acknowledge and assess it. In *100 Days to a Healthier Church*, I shared this example: "If someone in the church tells you they shared their faith with a friend for the first time, write that in the log. Was there a couple on the verge of divorce whose relationship was restored into a stronger marriage? Write that down. Was there someone who was resisting necessary change in the church but has decided maybe some changes aren't so bad after all? Write that down."[3]

The logs can be physical books, electronic spreadsheets, or whatever works for each member of the group. There's more help for this at karlvaters.com/church-health-assessment.

After six months to a year (I recommend a full year, allowing you to assess all the church's seasonal events), the group should review their Healthy Church Logs, setting aside any events, systems, or meetings that didn't score well. This is not about fixing problems; it's about discovering strengths. Compare your scores, paying special attention to the highest combined scores, then ask yourselves, "What do these have in common?" You're looking for trends and common threads—anything that might give you clues as to what your church's underlying strengths might be. And don't be afraid to think differently. One church might discover that they work well with at-risk youth, another might notice that they're great at hospitality, while another might uncover a hidden skill for encouraging and supporting artistic expression.

If everyone is assessing it honestly, the combined results can give you something accurate and objective, without defaulting to attendance figures.

Chapter 16

De-sizing
Evangelicalism

People say we're tearing down the church. I think
we're tearing down the stages.

K. J. RAMSEY

In Fishlake National Forest, Utah, there is a forest of aspen trees named Pando. But Pando is more than a forest. The 47,000-plus trees share the same DNA, linked by a common root system, making Pando the world's most massive single organism.[1] And it's dying. The smaller saplings are being eaten by cattle and wild animals. This has led to a far greater concentration of older, larger trees, but not nearly enough smaller, younger saplings. The big are getting bigger, the small are disappearing, and this is killing the entire organism.

The comparisons to modern evangelicalism are so obvious and numerous it almost feels redundant to state them. But I will. Like Pando, the church is not multiple organisms, but a single organism, with a common DNA and root system. What affects one part affects all parts. This is why we must de-size and de-individualize our approach to the body of Christ. Imagine if, in Pando, one "tree" started rising above the others to an outsized degree. We would probably want to celebrate the life that was evident in it. But, knowing the interconnectedness of Pando, we would be wise to study exactly why this tree was growing so fast and big, especially if the trees around it were shrinking or dying. Maybe it's growing because it's in a spot to receive more sun, more water, and other forms of life-giving nutrition. If so, we should study it, learn from it, and apply its principles to the rest of Pando. Or perhaps it's a parasite, sucking the life out of the others to sustain its own growth. If so, not only is it not benefiting the entire organism, but it's also an existential threat.

In American evangelicalism, there are those who automatically assume the growing church is doing something right, while the smaller churches are doing something wrong. There are also those who make the opposite assumption—that the growing church is always a parasite feeding off the others and damaging the whole. In reality, there are churches of both types, in all sizes.

As long as we keep seeing each congregation as an individual tree instead of one shoot from a common root system, we will fail to ask the right questions. And we'll miss answers that may be very simple.

Reconsider the Prevailing
Church Growth Hypothesis

When scientists propose an idea, they start by writing a hypothesis. *If you combine X with Y, it will result in Z.* Then they conduct experiments to determine if their hypothesis is true, sharing the results with other scientists who run even more tests. It's a rigorous, sometimes tedious and discouraging process. But when it's done correctly, it can lead to a theory, an explanation for how something works that bears the weight of criticism. Experimentation and observation allow the hypothesis to either be proven false, or to become an idea that works in the real world.

For over forty years, the prevailing church growth hypothesis has been "all healthy things grow." Sometimes it's stated in the inverse as, "If you remove obstacles to growth, your church will grow." But I've never heard this presented as a hypothesis; I've only seen it presented as an irrefutable fact. But where's the evidence? At best, about 10 percent of churches seem to confirm the truth of those statements, while 90 percent have failed to produce similar results. If a scientific hypothesis was shown to produce negative results in 90 percent of experiments, we wouldn't refer to the 90 percent as failures; we'd refer to the hypothesis as a non-starter. Craig Van Gelder observes, "I have read few Church Growth studies that have used careful sampling procedures and sound controls to test hypotheses, although these methods are readily available from the social sciences."[2] This is especially disheartening when we know how committed Donald McGavran was to using the principles of research, peer-review, and the social sciences to discover universal Church Growth principles.

We need to reframe 90 percent of churches not as failures, but as experiments that have shown the "all healthy things grow" hypothesis to be, if not wrong, at least woefully incomplete. That might finally put us in the frame of mind to look for other solutions besides the relentless drive for bigger. Maybe then we'd be open to de-sizing the church. In 1995, Mark Noll raised eyebrows when he published *The Scandal of the Evangelical Mind*, in which he accused evangelicals of not thinking as deeply as we should about culture, the arts, and science. I believe there's also a scandal of the evangelical church-growth mind*set* that we need to take seriously.

Here are some ways to start de-sizing evangelicalism by reframing our mindset and our behaviors away from two generations of being obsessed with numbers:

Make "Responsive Design" Your Default

When designers create websites, they use a principle called responsive design. This is what causes webpages to automatically resize, depending on the screen you're using. Everything you see on a laptop is also there on your smart phone, but it's configured for the device. Responsive design is such an industry standard that no one would think of designing a website without using it. But when publishers, denominations, and curriculum developers create products for use in churches, they usually design them from a big church context. So, these products tend to work well in big churches and ministries with little thought as to how they might work differently in smaller congregations. This must change. Ironically, to de-size our curriculum, programs, conferences, and other leadership materials, we need to think *more* about the variations in church size, not less.

Have Small-Church Leaders in Every Stage of Planning

The best way to embed responsive design into everything we do is to collaborate with people from various church sizes on every step of the process. Whether you're a publisher who's writing curriculum, a parachurch ministry that's organizing a big leadership conference, or a denominational leader designing a program, at least one small-church leader should be on the planning team from concept to execution. Yes, we need pastors representing big churches too, but that happens in virtually every situation already. The missing ingredient for responsive design is small-church representation.

Promote Alternative Church Structures

There are church formats that don't follow the numbers-driven model, house churches being the most well-known and oldest of them. When I talk with house-church proponents, their biggest challenges are 1) finding a house church with biblical teaching, and 2) when they move to a new place, finding one at all. This is an opportunity for our existing church structures to work alongside alternative structures for the greater benefit of everyone.

What would happen if denominations and parachurch

organizations created their own house-church departments? They could work with house churches that already fit within their theological parameters, and they could start house churches of their own. Then, when someone moves to a new city and wants to find a house church that holds to those theological beliefs, they can check the denominational or parachurch website to find one near them. No, this would not be easy, and yes, I can already imagine many of the pitfalls along the way. But I think this is a huge opportunity that we need to take seriously.

Look for the Hand of God in Numerical Decline

We automatically assume that numerical decline in a church must be the sign of a problem. Most of the time it is. But sometimes it's God's way of shifting and sifting. In *God Meetings*, Dave Beckwith writes about serving in a very large church that began to follow the Body Life model pioneered at Peninsula Bible Church in Palo Alto, California. Their Sunday evening Body Life services "topped out at about five hundred in attendance but then began an alarming decline," eventually bottoming out at 125 (a number that nine out of ten churches would love to have, but a huge concern when it's only 25 percent of what it used to be).

Bob Smith, an associate pastor at Peninsula Bible, told Beckwith they had experienced an even steeper drop from 800 down to 150 (less than 20 percent of their highwater mark). The reason, Smith told Beckwith, was, "It finally became clear to us that Body Life—people sharing their lives, praying for one another, and being taught the Word—never stopped. It just changed locations. Rather than Body Life happening in a large audience, God moved it into small groups, which continue. *It took us a long time to see the hand of God in declining numbers.*"[3]

Yes, it's hard to see the hand of God in declining numbers. But sometimes that's exactly what it is. To know the difference, we have to look deeper.

Consider the Healthy Hundred

Pastor Jerry Riddle of Eagle Rock Church in Little Rock, Arkansas, wrote a letter to his small congregation a few years ago. In it, he admitted: "For 30 plus years of ministry life, I have been prone to consider mighty ministry in terms of 1,000s and 10,000s. You cannot possibly imagine the bouts of failure and disappointment I have occasionally discovered myself sinking into as I have consciously or subconsciously measured my life effectiveness in terms of 4- 5- and 6-digit attendance and salvation figures."

This is not an unusual burden for pastors to be under. What makes Jerry's experience different is how he has dealt with it. In his letter, he goes on to explain: "As of late I have begun to consider the prominence a Healthy Hundred could bring into our community, nation, and world. I cannot fathom the power, significance, and impact of such a band of believers. In fact, I am just beginning to genuinely realize the shake-up of a single, sold out, saint. The reality of a Healthy Hundred stretches well beyond my imagination."[4]

We need to let go of forms of church that are designed to gather large numbers and stay laser-focused on what Jesus called His church to do: make disciples.

Is the Healthy Hundred for everyone? Of course not. In many small towns, getting even a hundred people in the church would be huge. But the concept of asking "What would a church of one hundred healthy believers look like, and what steps could we take to get started on that journey?" is a much more viable way for a lot of churches to approach health and growth. It's worth considering.

Choose Forms That Promote Discipleship over Numerical Increase

Jesus said He would build His church, while He commands us to make disciples. So, we need to let go of forms of church that are designed to gather large numbers and stay laser-focused on what Jesus called His church to do: make disciples. Not crowds, not fans, not giving units, not even converts. Disciples. Any form that promotes discipleship is good; any form that doesn't is bad.

Simple? Yes. Simplistic? No. Easy? Not on your life. Necessary? Absolutely.

Consider the Minimum Viable Church

In 2011, Jim Collins and Jerry I. Porras wrote the book *Built to Last*. In it, they talked about the importance of businesses pursuing a Big Hairy Audacious Goal (BHAG).[5] Since then, I have heard no less than a dozen church leaders tell pastors they need to have a "B-HAG" as a necessary ingredient to build a great church. This is a prime example of our obsession with numbers in the church. Such advice may have inspired a few pastors to go on to bigger, more audacious things, but it seriously discouraged a generation of pastors who tried, but failed to even *think* of a BHAG that they truly felt the Lord was leading them toward.

Instead of dreaming big and hairy, let's reverse our thinking and take our bare minimums seriously. What is the smallest possible dream you have for a church you would want to be a part of? Not what people expect you to say, just the bare minimum expectation of what a church *should* be.

One way to think about it is to finish this sentence: When all my big, expensive dreams are laid aside, I just want to be a part of a church ...

195

- That helps me blossom in my God given gifts?
- With people who truly love Jesus and care about me?
- That lays aside the hype and doesn't feel fake?
- Where I won't be hurt again?

(Write your answer here)

If you asked the average churchgoer (and the average nonchurch-goer) what they're looking for in a church, most would pick one with a baseline of character, kindness, biblical teaching, worship, and ministry, not the one that's constantly pushing for goals that are Bigger! Hairier! More Audacious! BHAGs are great in the right context. But they're not necessary in most churches. The idea that every church and pastor *must* have one for viable ministry is nonsense.

Treat Sins Differently than Mistakes

When we're chasing bigness in the church, we develop a bad habit of treating mistakes as if they were sins, and sins as if they were merely mistakes. If someone in a position of authority sins, it's often swept under the rug so the machine can keep rolling. But if a department head makes a non-sinful mistake, they can find themselves on the end of a serious tongue-lashing or quickly removed from their position. When we do that, we create an unhealthy environment of secrecy in which people know they need to hide their mistakes so they won't get yelled at or fired, while knowing someone else can keep sinning as long as they keep it on the down-low and produce the desired numerical results. That probably sounds more cynical than I feel. It doesn't happen as often as cynics would suggest, but the fact that it happens often enough for most pastors to be able to point to examples of it means it happens way too much.

In many churches and parachurch ministries, the desire to mask our weaknesses and excuse our sins so we can keep the machine running creates an environment where the word "sin" isn't even allowed (as one church staff member told me, the senior leader referred to it only as "the S word"), let alone acknowledged and dealt with, even when it's egregious. Unless it becomes public. But even then, the public exposure is often seen as a mistake larger than the sin itself, leading to cover-ups, excuse-making, and scapegoating.

Be Quick to Restore, but Not to Re-platform

When a pastor has a moral failing, they need to leave the platform for a much longer time than they generally do. The rush to re-platform gifted speakers may be one of the most hurtful things the evangelical church does for fallen ministers. And it's always damaging to their victims, often revictimizing them. In many cases, the lure of the spotlight is such a contributing factor to the minister's fall that true restoration may mean removing them from the spotlight for good. For some people, the platform is an addiction. As gifted as they might be, they can't resist the lure of a stage any more than an alcoholic can resist the lure of a bar. Some sins disqualify people from platforms for good. This doesn't preclude the fallen leader from ministry, as long as it's behind the scenes, but the degree to which most restored ministers resist a non-spotlight role is a good indicator of how deeply they need to be de-sized, not re-platformed.

One type of disqualification is the narcissistic leader. According to Scot McKnight and Laura Barringer in *A Church Called Tov*, "it is common for a narcissist to want his church to be seen as the *best*, the *biggest*, and the *most influential* because he believes the glory belongs to the leader."[6] There's no evidence to suggest that big churches are more likely to be led by narcissistic pastors than small ones, but all narcissists want the stage, no matter how big or small it is. As Chuck DeGroat has noted, "I've known healthy large church pastors, even celebrity pastors, who empower rather than disempower. . . .

It's possible. But given my experience, I remain cautious whenever I hear about venerated 'star' pastors."[7]

Their caution is warranted. Given that the pursuit of bigness and celebrity is a common character trait of narcissists, we must pause and consider our true motives any time we're creating a culture that leans toward it, therefore normalizing some of the very traits that narcissists are attracted to. These narcissistic goals don't just stop with the pastor. Once they entrench themselves in a church culture, as DeGroat notes, they can prompt "a collective sense of pride that God is blessing us (and *not* that church across the street). This phenomenon is sometimes called 'collective narcissism.'"[8] This is why church health must be the number one priority. "Healthy churches simply do not hire narcissistic pastors," DeGroat tells us. "They can spot one a mile away."[9]

> **"Can they draw a crowd?" needs to disappear from the questions we ask when considering whether someone is called to pastor.**

Platform Quality over Quantity

"Can they draw a crowd?" needs to disappear from the questions we ask when considering whether someone is called to pastor. It's impossible to focus on the quality of a person's character, the strength of their calling, and their spiritual maturity when numbers get involved. Yes, *impossible*. Numbers have such a hold over us that the moment they're in the mix, all other factors fade into the background. Plus, look at the qualifications for leadership in the Bible. From Jethro's advice for Moses, to Jesus' teachings, to Paul's advice for Timothy and Titus,[10] all the biblical qualifications for leaders are about character, while none—literally *none* of them—are about drawing a crowd.

Quality isn't the *most important* thing; it's the *only* thing that matters. When anything else gets into the mix, it gets very dangerous, very quickly.

Promote Content over Celebrity

Platforming popular speakers will give you a bigger audience, but at what cost? It's not worth the immediate crowd or clicks when it reinforces the ethereal and toxic celebrity culture. Creating and promoting quality content won't get you as big an audience, but it's more likely to endure.

What's Coming Next?

What might the church look like if we started de-sizing? I'm not naïve or foolish enough to predict anything. But I do believe we can look at several trends that are already in the works and extend them into the future to imagine what a de-sized church might look like.

Decentralized Leadership

The history of the world is, in many ways, a tug of war between networks and hierarchies. In churches, the heyday of hierarchical power is waning, and fast. It will never leave entirely (history has proven that), but for the next several generations, interlinked networks of like-minded people are more likely to be the lines along which churches form, are sustained, and will either succeed or fail.

In *The Square and the Tower*, Niall Ferguson describes what happens historically when networks and hierarchies clash. "When a distributed network attacks a hierarchy, the hierarchy reacts in the ways that come naturally to it."[11] What comes naturally to a hierarchy is more hierarchy. Right now, the hierarchical nature of the church is under assault. Our gut reaction may be to circle the wagons, expel the infidels, and protect our structures. But that's not the right approach.

As Ferguson notes, "A hierarchy is a clumsy tool to use against a network. . . . The kind of networks we need can't be formed or sustained through coercive comments about being 'with us' or 'against us.'"[12] The church must work together. This is the way Jesus designed His church, after all. With no ultimate authority other than Christ Himself, just a network of disciples making disciples. Doubling down on hierarchical structures will not save the church or reach the next generation. Only the body of Christ, honoring and using all its parts, is fit to meet this challenge.

Post-denominational Confusion

We live in a post-denominational era. Denominations are still with us, and they have an important role to play, but they are no longer the primary way people identify their faith. This is a good trend. After all, we're called to make disciples, not more members of our little tribe.

But the church will not undergo a full transition into a post-denominational culture without significant pain, frustration, and confusion. We're seeing it in almost all major denominations right now, with some splitting over essential doctrines, while others are almost coming to blows over points of theology that used to be (and still *should* be) secondary. These rising denominational disputes are probably the loud but dying gasps of a soon-to-be-lost paradigm for how churches connect, identify, and hold each other accountable.

We don't know what will come in their wake, but it will likely repair some of denominationalism's faults, while creating a new set of problems that no one has considered yet.

Less Focus on Facilities

When most church planters think about starting a church, the first thing they want to do is find a building. When the average church-goer talks about church, they think about the building first, the mission second. When we fight in churches, too many of our arguments are over the building. When we raise money, far too much of it goes into the building. Even when we think about how God meets us in worship, we often imagine God's presence entering a building, more than abiding with His people.

New generations appear to have less focus on facilities than previous generations had. This is good. We need to applaud and promote that kind of thinking. De-sizing the church will mean—and it *must* include—de-emphasizing the number of people in the building in favor of re-emphasizing the mission that happens after we leave the building.

There are some positive steps already happening in this direction. Most megachurches have gone multi-venue and multisite, preferring several smaller gatherings to a single massive one. I've even consulted with multisite pastors about how to reframe their thinking when they're on staff at a big church but are responsible for pastoring a smaller group on their church campus.

A Renewed Appreciation for the Church's Long Tail

Small churches are the engine that drives the body of Christ around the world. It's not that big churches don't play an important role. They certainly do. But the role of small churches can't be denied either.

"The long tail" is a phrase coined by Chris Anderson in *Wired* magazine in 2004. It's the economic concept that, while most people are enamored with products that sell in massive numbers, there's just as big a market for the millions of niche products.

It's called the long tail because, when represented as a graph, it starts as a big spike on the left, signifying a very small number of products (on the x-axis) with massive sales (on the y-axis), then it drops quickly so that most of the space on the graph is taken up by a slowly fading line that crawls along the bottom of the x-axis like a long tail. That tail represents the vast number of products that sell in small amounts.

While those products don't sell a lot on their own, there are so many of them that the total number of products sold equals—or is sometimes greater than—the hits.

Here's how the long tail works in business. According to Chris Anderson, "The average Barnes & Noble carries 130,000 titles. Yet more than half of Amazon's book sales come from outside its top 130,000 titles. The market for books that are too small to be stocked in the average bookstore is larger than the market for those that are."[13]

The long tail phenomenon can be seen in the church, as well. We tend to notice and celebrate the small percentage of churches that are large and growing fast (the big spike on the y-axis) almost exclusively, but there are as many people attending, worshiping, ministering, and sharing their faith in small churches (the long tail on the x-axis) because there are so many more churches there. YouTube, Amazon, and Apple have built some of the biggest businesses on earth by capitalizing on the value of the long tail. The average customer notices the viral videos, bestselling books, and thousand-dollar phones, but the businesses know there's as much of an audience for their huge catalog of small items (homemade videos, self-published books, and iTunes songs) as there is for the larger items.

The long tail may be a new term, but it's an old idea. It's the way the church has always done ministry. The church thrives on massive numbers of small churches ministering to millions of people.

Unfortunately, just like many people ignore small businesses in favor of massive corporations, too much of our current church leadership teaching does the same. We ignore, or belittle, the millions of small churches to favor the big ones. The truth is, just like businesses need both bestsellers and niche products, the church has always been at its most effective when it honors both small and large congregations, not one to the exclusion of the other.

Small congregations are the church's long tail. They're just as needed as big churches, but they're often not recognized for the value they bring. It's time for that to change. Along with big churches, the long tail of small churches needs to be recognized, embraced, celebrated, and resourced.

Abandon the "Jesus Junk"

In 2012, Skye Jethani coined the phrase, "the Evangelical Industrial Complex," in an article for *Christianity Today* to describe the tendency for us to celebrate, platform, and promote pastors of large churches almost exclusively in books, conferences, and as examples to follow.[14] It was a spin on Dwight Eisenhower's phrase "the Military Industrial Complex," which he warned the nation about in his 1961 farewell address to the nation. When I was first made aware of Jethani's phrase, I was skeptical. It felt overblown and cynical to me. Not anymore. I've come to believe that this phrase is compellingly strong and possibly prophetic.

In the late 1970s, musician Keith Green used an even shorter, blunter term, referring to the selling of everything from Christian T-shirts and breath mints to his own records (which he famously decided to give away for free—along with admission to his concerts) as "Jesus Junk."

> We go from glorifying musicians in the world, to glorifying Christian musicians. It's all idolatry! Can't you see that? It's true that there are many men and women of God who are greatly anointed to call down the Spirit of God on His people and the unsaved. But Satan is getting a great victory as we seem to worship these ministers on tapes and records, and clamor to get their autographs in churches and concert halls from coast to coast.[15]

Lesslie Newbigin might have had Eisenhower's warning in mind when he cautioned us about this in 1978, writing: "When numerical growth is taken as the criterion of judgment on the church, we are transported with alarming ease into the world of the military campaign or the commercial sales drive."[16]

Evangelicalism might survive, possibly under a different name and only with many necessary de-sizing reforms. But the Evangelical Industrial Complex is not a good idea that can be reimagined. It's a bad idea that must be abandoned to float away on the tide with all the other "junk."

Famous in Heaven

In *The Great Divorce*, C. S. Lewis draws a beautiful picture of the difference between what we value and what heaven values. In this work of fiction, the protagonist arrives at the outskirts of paradise and is trying to take it all in. Being guided by one of Lewis's literary heroes (George McDonald with a heavy Scottish brogue), he sees a huge procession arriving, honoring a woman. Assuming it's Mary, the mother of Jesus, he falters in his speaking:

> "Is it? . . . is it?" I whispered to my guide.
> "Not at all," said he. "It's someone ye'll never have heard of. Her name on earth was Sarah Smith and she lived at Golders Green."
> "She seems to be . . . well, a person of particular importance?"
> "Aye. She is one of the great ones. Ye have heard that fame in this country and fame on Earth are two quite different things."[17]

No, it's not Mary. And, in fact, Lewis never says the protagonist thinks it's Mary. That's an assumption Lewis leads us to make, but he never states it outright. The protagonist could have been expecting anyone he admired. For a writer of Lewis's skill, this has to be intentional. Today, we might imagine our favorite high-profile pastor, author, or celebrity as someone worthy of such honor. Instead, one of the greatest people in heaven is a simple woman who gained no earthly notoriety. This passage of Lewis's resonates so deeply because we've all met people like Sarah Smith who live with simple integrity. And when we pause to ask who is truly worthy of the greatest admiration, they are the ones we recall. Not the famous preacher, the online influencer, and certainly not the author you're reading right now. It's the person who may only be known to you and a handful of other people.

All my life I have been surrounded by people of exceptional integrity. My wife, my parents, my siblings, my children, my church leadership, and so many others. Most people have not had that blessing, but my experience should not be so rare. Living, working, and worshiping with people who are fundamentally honest and kind should not be exceptional, it should be normal. And in the church, it should be our hallmark.

Fame in heaven and on earth are quite different.

We know this. We need to remember it. And live it.

De-sizing starts here.

———

The Church Health Assessment Tool

It's free, it's fast, and it's not about attendance.
Also available at KarlVaters.com/Church-Health-Assessment.

In your congregation right now, how true are the following statements?

0 – Not at all
1 – Almost never
2 – Seldom
3 – Somewhat
4 – Very
5 – Always

Enter a score in the blank for each statement.

THEOLOGY

Bible

_____ The eternal truths of the Bible are taught well and applied to our lives in practical ways.

Worship

_____ Worship through song, prayer, and action is an essential focus of our congregation.

Salvation

_____ People are coming to faith in Jesus through the ministry of our church.

Discipleship

_____ Church members are growing in their faith, volunteering for ministry, and discipling others.

_____

THEOLOGY SUBTOTAL

LEADERSHIP

Teamwork

_____ There are more teams than committees because church members care more about doing ministry than having a title.

Unity

_____ There is a strong sense of love, cooperation, and friendship among church members.

Alignment

_____ There is a high degree of communication, cooperation, and respect among department and ministry leaders.

Contextualization

_____ The language and methods we use to communicate the gospel can be easily grasped by an unchurched person.

_____

LEADERSHIP SUBTOTAL

MISSION

First Impressions

_____ There is an effective process in place to help first-time guests feel welcome and get connected.

Outreach

_____ Congregation members feel good about telling their friends about the church and inviting them to attend.

Demographics

_____ The demographic mix of our congregation (race, gender, age, etc.) is at least as diverse as our neighborhood.

Impact

_____ If our church closed tomorrow, people outside our congregation would miss us.

_____

MISSION SUBTOTAL

ATTITUDE

Creativity

_____ When church members have new ministry ideas, they feel comfortable expressing them because they are heard, respected, and embraced.

Resilience

_____ Our church is a good place to ask hard questions because doubts aren't deadly, and failure isn't fatal.

Enthusiasm

_____ It's not unusual to see church members come early, stay late, sit up front, and volunteer when needed.

Anticipation

_____ We are more excited about the future than the past.

_____

ATTITUDE SUBTOTAL

_____

TOTAL SCORE

How Did You Do?

Above 70: Spectacular! This is a very healthy church. If your low scores are concentrated in one of the subtotal areas, work on that. Otherwise, keep building on your strengths.

50s–60s: Good. You have some work to do, but there's probably no emergency. If most of your low scores come from one or two subtotals, deal with those areas first.

30s–40s: Trouble. You need outside help from a denominational team or church leadership advisor. If you don't get help soon, your church is in danger of collapse.

Below 40: You may be in The Big Rut or The Death Rattle (chapter 7). If you have assets, this may be the time to sell them and make them available to a ministry that is strong.

There's some helpful and hopeful information about how to start doing that in *The Church Recovery Guide*, chapter 8 ("Closing a Congregation: Proactive Options for Dying Churches").

Acknowledgments

A s this book was in its final editing phase, two landmark events occurred in my life. One was planned, the other was a shock. The planned event was the end of my thirty-one years on the pastoral staff of Cornerstone Christian Fellowship: twenty-five as lead pastor, six as teaching pastor. The ministry of Helping Small Churches Thrive has been growing every year and now requires our full attention. Cornerstone remains Shelley's and my home church where we continue to worship, learn, and grow. In fact, they are sending us out as their missionary representatives to help churches in need.

The other event was the surprisingly fast illness and passing of a good friend and mentor, Ron Cook. Ron and his wife, Jean, joined our church in 1961, the year it was planted under its founding pastor, Walter Price. Later, Ron was the chairman of the pastoral search team that brought me in as their pastor in 1992, after a decade of short-term pastorates had left the church very close to collapse. Over the following three-plus decades, Ron supported the church and me in innumerable ways with the kind of wisdom, godly discipleship, and integrity that I described in chapters 12 and 13. That the end of Ron's time with us would happen in the same month as the end of my time on the Cornerstone staff bears the tragic beauty of an epic poem. Ron Cook was our church's Sarah Smith from Golders Green, with no fame on earth. He is now famous in heaven.

I am grateful to Ron and his dear wife Jean, who with so many others at Cornerstone—including Gary and Ami Garcia and the entire leadership team—have supported Shelley and me in so many ways, including releasing us to follow the Lord into new areas of ministry.

I'm profoundly indebted to Saturday mornings at Brot Coffee Co. with my extended family for a soft place to land when life gets frantic. The support of my parents, sisters, and their families on a weekly basis means so much.

Mostly, I thank God for Shelley, our children, and the newest additions of Connor and Abigail, our grandchildren, who light up the room every time they enter it.

Notes

Introduction

Epigraph: Tim Suttle, *Shrink: Faithful Ministry in a Church-Growth Culture* (Grand Rapids, MI: Zondervan, 2014), Kindle loc. 539.

1. Darvin Wallis, "The Modern Evangelical Church Is Sick. Here's Where It Fell Apart," *Christian Post*, February 27, 2021, https://www.christianpost.com/voices/the-modern-evangelical-church-is-sick-where-it-fell-apart.html.

2. In *The Rise & Fall of Mars Hill* podcast, Ep. 6, is this conversation (starting at 64:45):

   Mike Cosper: I think it's pretty clear that Mark's investment in a place like TGC was really about helping him with the credibility he needed for the next level of influence he was after. And whenever issues came up in his life or in his ministry or his relationships, when people would push back at him and encourage him to submit to some older leaders around him, he wasn't shy about telling people why he didn't feel like he could submit to any of those men. I've heard it from multiple people that I interviewed.

   Collin Hansen: "I can't learn anything from a pastor whose church is smaller than 10,000 people."

   Mike Cosper: When he parted ways with Rick McKinley several years before, he said essentially the same thing.

   Rick McKinley: Our last real communication between Mark and I, I said, man, my hope for you is that you would find somebody to submit to. I said, I don't care if it's Piper or somebody, but you need to find somebody to submit to.

   And he said, I can't submit to Piper because my church is bigger than his. And I thought, we're [pause] I don't know where that kind of thinking comes from.

3. Ruth Malhotra, "Andy Stanley Explains His 'Stinking Selfish' Parents Comment," CT Online, March 8, 2016, https://www.christianitytoday.com/ct/2016/march-web-only/megachurch-pastor-andy-stanley-explains-contro versial-remar.html.

4. Ibid.

5. Taylor Berglund, "Pastor Perry Noble Fired After 16 Years at NewSpring Church," *Charisma News*, July 10, 2016 (italics mine).

6. "Who Killed Mars Hill? - Episode 1 - The Rise and Fall of Mars Hill," Christianity Today, YouTube (starts 17:50), https://youtu.be/4Cou36nSmJY?si=Ucr6zWhR8oPhbFG4.

7. David P. Cassidy's Twitter feed from August 3, 2021, https://twitter.com/DPCassidyTKC/status/1422685551061356544.

Chapter 1: The Danger of Idolizing Outcomes

Epigraph: Dallas Willard, *The Great Omission* (Old Saybrook, CT: ChristianAudio.com, 2007), Audiobook Chapter 6, 1:24:45.

1. Todd Wilson, *Multipliers: Leading Beyond Addition*, (Emeryville, CA: Exponential, 2017), 42 (emphasis mine).

2. Ibid., 24 (emphasis mine).

3. Ibid., 25 (emphasis mine).

4. Viktor E. Frankl, *Man's Search for Meaning* (Boston: Beacon Press, 2006), Kindle loc. 80.

Chapter 2: When Bigger Is the Enemy of Better

Epigraph: Kent and Barbara Hughes, *Liberating Ministry from the Success Syndrome* (Wheaton, IL: Crossway, 1987), 37.

1. Howard Schultz, *Pour Your Heart into It: How Starbucks Built a Company One Cup at a Time* (New York: Hachette Books, 1999), 146.

2. Tim Suttle, *Shrink: Faithful Ministry in a Church-Growth Culture* (Grand Rapids, MI: Zondervan, 2014), Kindle, loc. 304, 310, 317, and 330.

3. Dallas Willard, *The Great Omission*, (Old Saybrook, CT: ChristianAudio.com, 2007), Audiobook Chapter 5, 1:11:45.

4. JR Woodward and Dan White Jr., *The Church as Movement: Starting and Sustaining Missional-Incarnational Communities* (Downers Grove, IL: IVP Books, 2016), 56.

5. Philippians 4:8.

6. Graham Heslop, "Pastor, Why Do You Want a Big Church?," TGC Africa Edition, December 17, 2021, https://africa.thegospelcoalition.org/article/pastor-why-do-you-want-a-big-church/.

Chapter 3: Original Intent: Donald McGavran's Big Idea

Epigraph: Francis Chan, *Letters to the Church* (Colorado Springs, CO: David C. Cook, 2018), Kindle loc. 1997.

1. Nelson Searcy, from the foreword to Gary L. McIntosh, *Donald A. McGavran: A Biography of the Twentieth Century's Premiere Missiologist* (New York: Church Leader Insights USA, 2016), 7.

2. Elmer Towns, "Chapter 1: Effective Evangelism View," in *Evaluating the Church Growth Movement: Five Views*, Gary L. McIntosh, gen. ed., Peter E. Engle, series ed. (Grand Rapids, MI: Zondervan, 2004), 36–37.

3. George G. Hunter III, "The Legacy of Donald A. McGavran," *International Bulletin of Mission Research* 16, no. 4 (October 1992): https://journals.sagepub.com/doi/10.1177/239693939201600404.

4. Towns, "Chapter 1: Effective Evangelism View," 36.

5. Gary L. McIntosh, *Donald A. McGavran: A Biography of the Twentieth-Century's Premiere Missiologist* (New York: Church Leader Insights USA, 2016), 274, 138.

6. Thom Rainer, *The Book of Church Growth: History, Theology and Principles* (Nashville, TN: Broadman Press, 1993), 21.

7. Ibid., 36–37.

8. Rainer, *The Book of Church Growth*, 53.

9. McIntosh, *Donald A. McGavran*, 185.

10. Rainer, *The Book of Church Growth*, 53.

11. Wilbert R. Shenk, ed., *Exploring Church Growth* (Eugene, OR: Wipf and Stock, 1983), 85.

12. Rick Warren, *The Purpose Driven Church: Growth Without Compromising Your Message & Mission* (Grand Rapids, MI: Zondervan, 1995), 29.

13. McIntosh, *Donald A. McGavran*, 15.

14. Gary L. McIntosh, "The Church Growth Movement and Small Churches: A Conversation," Sin Boldly podcast with Evan McClanahan, 15:22, https://www.youtube.com/watch?v=qUu6UGfqGlg&t=922s.

15. Ibid., 16:39.

16. McIntosh, *Donald A. McGavran*, 274.

17. Charles Van Engen, "Chapter 3: Centrist View," in *Evaluating the Church Growth Movement: Five Views*, Gary L. McIntosh, gen. ed., Peter E. Engle, series ed. (Grand Rapids, MI: Zondervan, 2004), 194.

18. Harvie M. Conn, "Chapter 7. Looking for a Method: Backgrounds and Suggestions," Wilbert R. Shenk, ed., in *Exploring Church Growth* (Eugene, OR: Wipf and Stock, 1983), 79.

19. McIntosh, *Donald A. McGavran*, 15.

Chapter 4: (Pre)Made in America

Epigraph: Tim Suttle, *Shrink: Faithful Ministry in a Church-Growth Culture* (Grand Rapids, MI: Zondervan, 2014), Kindle loc. 357.

1. Wanjiru M. Gitau, *Megachurch Christianity Reconsidered: Millennials and Social Change in African Perspective* (Downers Grove, IL: IVP Academic, 2018), 112.

2. Ibid., 153.

3. *Encyclopedia Britannica*, "Pirates, Privateers, Corsairs, Buccaneers: What's the Difference?," September 18, 2017, https://www.britannica.com/story/pirates-privateers-corsairs-buccaneers-whats-the-difference.

4. On their way to the colonies, they had raided a Portuguese slave ship with 350 Africans aboard, seizing twenty for themselves, who they now brought with them. Slavery was not new to the continent since some Europeans had already brought enslaved people with them. What was distinctly tragic about this moment is that it didn't merely perpetuate the evil of existing slavery, which would have been bad enough, but it was the start of building an entire culture and economy based on it.

5. Olivia B. Waxman, "The First Africans in Virginia Landed in 1619. It Was a Turning Point for Slavery in American History—But Not the Beginning," Time.com, August 20, 2019, https://time.com/5653369/august-1619-jamestown-history.

6. "The Bill of Rights: A Transcription," *National Archives*, https://www.archives.gov/founding-docs/bill-of-rights-transcript.

7. Tod Bolsinger, *Canoeing the Mountains: Christian Leadership in Uncharted Territory* (Downers Grove, IL: IVP Books, 2015), 88.

8. Susan Cain, *Quiet: The Power of Introverts in a World That Can't Stop Talking* (New York: Crown, 2012), 30.

9. Frances FitzGerald, *The Evangelicals: The Struggle to Shape America* (New York: Simon & Schuster, 2017), 25.

10. Ibid., 43–44.

11. Ibid., 37–38, 43.

12. Glenn Packiam, *The Resilient Pastor: Leading Your Church in a Rapidly Changing World* (Grand Rapids, MI: Baker Books, 2022), 130.

13. "About D. L. Moody," D. L. Moody Center, https://moodycenter.org/about-the-moody-center/about-d-l-moody/.

14. David Maas, "The Life & Times of D. L. Moody," *Christianity Today*, https://www.christianitytoday.com/history/issues/issue-25/life-times-of-d-l-moody.html.

15. Wendy Knickerbocker, "Billy Sunday," *Society for American Baseball Research*, https://sabr.org/bioproj/person/billy-sunday/.

16. FitzGerald, *The Evangelicals*, 13.

17. "In Western European Countries with Church Taxes, Support for the Tradition Remains Strong," April 30, 2019, Pew Research Center, https://www.pewresearch.org/religion/2019/04/30/in-western-european-countries-with-church-taxes-support-for-the-tradition-remains-strong.

18. Contract Clause, Legal Information Institute, Cornell Law School, https://www.law.cornell.edu/constitution-conan/article-1/section-10/clause-1/contract-clause.

19. Nathan O. Hatch, *The Democratization of American Christianity* (New Haven, CT: Yale University Press, 1991), Kindle 67.

20. Winn Collier, *A Burning in My Bones: The Authorized Biography of Eugene H. Peterson, Translator of The Message* (Colorado Springs, CO: WaterBrook, 2021), Kindle edition, 123–24.

21. Ibid.

22. Scot McKnight and Laura Barringer, *A Church Called Tov: Forming a Goodness Culture That Resists Abuses of Power and Promotes Healing* (Carol Stream, IL: Tyndale, 2020), 201.

23. Ibid., 203 (emphasis in the original).

24. Skye Jethani, *Immeasurable: Reflections on the Soul of Ministry in the Age of Church, Inc.*, (Chicago: Moody, 2017), Kindle loc. 1693, 1696. (Jethani cites *The Churching of America, 1776–1990*, by Roger Finke and Rodney Stark, as his source.)

25. George Washington, in his letter to Catharine Sawbridge Macaulay Graham, New York, January 9, 1790, https://founders.archives.gov/documents/Washington/05-04-02-0363.

Chapter 5: The Streams Combine

Epigraph: Most commonly attributed to Francis Bacon, https://quotefancy.com/quote/805422. Cotton Mather referred to it as "that old observation" in his *Magnalia Christi Americana*, translating it from the Latin as "Religion brought forth Prosperity, and the *daughter* destroyed the *mother*" (italics and capital P in the original), https://books.google.com/books?id=49JdS7NoSawC&printsec=frontcover&dq=Magnalia+Christi+Americana#v=onepage&q=Magnalia%20Christi%20Americana&f=false.

1. Gary L. McIntosh, *Donald A. McGavran: A Biography of the Twentieth-Century's Premiere Missiologist* (New York: Church Leader Insights USA, 2016), 43.

2. Rich Karlgaard, "Purpose Driven," *Forbes*, February 16, 2004, https://www.forbes.com/forbes/2004/0216/039.html.

3. Rick Warren, *The Purpose Driven Church: Growth Without Compromising Your Message & Mission* (Grand Rapids, MI: Zondervan, 1995), 29.

4. Ibid., 30.

5. Charles R. Taber, "Chapter 10: Contextualization," in *Exploring Church Growth*, ed. Wilbert R. Shenk (Eugene, OR: Wipf and Stock, 1983), 125.

Chapter 6: Boom: The Impact of Suburbs on the Church

Epigraph: Susan Cain, *Quiet: The Power of Introverts in a World That Can't Stop Talking* (New York: Crown, 2012), 21-22.

1. James Wellman Jr., Katie Corcoran, and Kate Stockly, *High on God: How Megachurches Won the Heart of America* (Oxford, England: Oxford University Press, 2020), Kindle loc. 1027.

2. Ibid., Kindle loc. 1226.

3. According to a 1927 article, "Some Facts About the Moody Church," the original building had "2,200 seats in the main floor and 1,840 in the balcony," Moody Media, https://www.moodymedia.org/articles/some-facts-about-the-moody-church/.

4. "The Angelus Temple," PBS.org, https://www.pbs.org/wgbh/americanexperience/features/sister-angelus-temple/.

5. According to Warren Bird in the article "World's First Megachurch?," the first book containing the word "megachurch" was *How Churches Grow in an Urban World* by Francis M. DuBose, published in 1978, https://leadnet.org/worlds_first_megachurch/.

6. Scott Thumma and Dave Travis, *Beyond Megachurch Myths: What We Can Learn From America's Largest Churches*, 6-7.

7. Aaron Earls, "Megachurches Continue to (Mostly) Grow and Not Just in Size," December 15, 2020, Lifeway.com, https://research.lifeway.com/2020/12/15/megachurches-continue-to-mostly-grow-and-not-just-in-size.

8. Thumma and Travis, *Beyond Megachurch Myths*, 11.

9. "The Great Migration (1910–1970)," National Archives, https://www.archives.gov/research/african-americans/migrations/great-migration.

10. Frank Jacobs, "Marchetti's Constant: The Curious Principle That Shapes Our Cities," Big Think, https://bigthink.com/strange-maps/marchettis-constant.

11. Tom Standage, *A Brief History of Motion: From the Wheel, to the Car, to What Comes Next* (London: Bloomsbury Publishing, 2021), Kindle loc. 1944.

12. Originally named "parkways" after the broad horse-cart paths through parks, then because the wide roadways were initially built to ease cramped inner-city life by giving families access to out-of-town parks on the weekend. "Why Do We Park in the Driveway and Drive on the Parkway?" Merriam-Webster. https://www.merriam-webster.com/wordplay/drive-parkway-park-driveway-history

13. "A Quick History of the Supermarket," July 4, 2009, https://www.groceteria.com/about/a-quick-history-of-the-supermarket.

14. Wanjiru M. Gitau, *Megachurch Christianity Reconsidered: Millennials and Social Change in African Perspective* (Downers Grove, IL: IVP Academic, 2018), 157.

15. Peter Smith, "America's Nonreligious Are a Growing, Diverse Phenomenon. They Really Don't Like Organized Religion," *The Associated Press*, October 4, 2023, https://apnews.com/article/nonreligious-united-states-nones-spirituality-humanist-91bb8430280c88fd88530a7ad64b03f8.

Chapter 7: Inevitable: Why the Christian Celebrity Culture Guarantees Moral Failure

Epigraph 1: Beth Moore, Twitter thread, 3.30.2022, https://twitter.com/BethMooreLPM/status/1509158050078375941.

Epigragh 2: Carl Lentz, sitting for an interview in the last seconds of *The Secrets of Hillsong*, Season 1, Ep. 1.

1. Sharon Marcus (Orlando Harriman Professor of English and Comparative Literature at Columbia University, and the author of *The Drama of Celebrity*), as interviewed in "The Long and Strange History of Celebrity," *Columbia Magazine*, Fall 2019, https://magazine.columbia.edu/article/long-and-strange-history-celebrity.

2. Ibid.

3. John Kobler, in his article, "Bernhardt in America," *American Heritage,* July/August 1989, wrote, "During Sarah Bernhardt's 1912–13 American tour, the souvenir program for La Dame aux Camélias quoted Mark Twain: 'There are five kinds of actresses: bad actresses, fair actresses, good actresses, great actresses, and Sarah Bernhardt,'" https://www.americanheritage.com/bernhardt-america.

4. Jethani, *Immeasurable*, Kindle loc. 1482.

5. Katelyn Beaty, *Celebrities for Jesus: How Personas, Platforms, and Profits are Hurting the Church* (Grand Rapids, MI: Brazos Press, 2022), 17.

6. Ibid., 19.

7. Paul David Tripp, *Dangerous Calling: Confronting the Unique Challenges of Pastoral Ministry* (Wheaton IL: Crossway, 2012), 157.

8. Stacey Lee, as quoted by David Smith in "'Why Do Pastors Keep Falling?': Inside the Shocking Downfall of Hillsong Church," May 18, 2023, https://www.theguardian.com/tv-and-radio/2023/may/18/hillsong-church-documentary-carl-lentz-scandal (italics mine).

9. Daniel Darling's Twitter feed, https://twitter.com/dandarling/status/1659967868627308545.

10. Chris Galanos, *From Megachurch to Multiplication: A Church's Journey Toward Movement* (Experience Life, 2018), Kindle loc. 898.

11. Jethani, *Immeasurable*, Kindle loc. 431, 432, 438.

12. Katie Jo Ramsey, *The Lord Is My Courage: Stepping Through the Shadows of Fear Toward the Voice of Love* (Grand Rapids, MI: Zondervan reflective, 2022), Kindle loc. 1183.

13. "MBWA Meaning: Tips for Management by Walking Around," MasterClass, April 4, 2022, https://www.masterclass.com/articles/mbwa.

14. Les McKeown on the Carey Nieuwhof Leadership Podcast, *CNLP 112: Les McKeown on Getting Your Church or Organization into a Place of Predictable Success,* https://careynieuwhof.com/episode112/ (starting at 44:42).

15. Scot McKnight and Laura Barringer, *A Church Called Tov: Forming a Goodness Culture that Resists Abuses of Power and Promotes Healing.* (Carol Stream, IL: Tyndale, 2020), 198.

Chapter 8: What the Church Growth Movement Got Right

Epigraph: Thom Rainer, *The Book of Church Growth: History, Theology and Principles* (Nashville, TN: Broadman Press, 1993), 177.

1. James Wellman Jr., Katie Corcoran, and Kate Stockly, *High on God: How Megachurches Won the Heart of America* (Oxford, England: Oxford University Press, 2020), Kindle loc. 773.

2. Scott Thumma, "Exploring the Megachurch Phenomena: Their Characteristics and Cultural Context," Hartford Institute for Religion Research, http://hirr .hartsem.edu/bookshelf/thumma_article2.html.

Chapter 9: Where the Church Growth Movement Went Sideways

Epigraph: Elmer Towns, "Chapter 1: Effective Evangelism View," *Evaluating the Church Growth Movement: Five Views*, Gary L. McIntosh, gen. ed., Peter E. Engle, series ed. (Grand Rapids, MI: Zondervan, 2004), 47.

1. From Towns's bio in *Evaluating the Church Growth Movement: Five Views*, 274.

2. Towns, "Chapter 1: Effective Evangelism View," *Evaluating the Church Growth Movement: Five Views*, 52.

3. Jon Krakauer, *Into Thin Air: A Personal Account of the Mount Everest Disaster* (New York, NY: Villard Books, 1997).

4. Todd Wilson, *Multipliers: Leading Beyond Addition.*, (Emeryville, CA: Exponential, 2017), 59.

5. Gary McIntosh, *One Size Doesn't Fit All: Bringing Out the Best in Any Size Church* (Grand Rapids, MI: Baker Books, 1999), 114.

6. Wilson, *Multipliers*, 58.

7. Winn Collier, *A Burning in My Bones: The Authorized Biography of Eugene H. Peterson, Translator of The Message* (Colorado Springs: WaterBrook, 2021), Kindle edition, 271.

8. From the Willow Creek archives, "From The Beginning . . . Reach Your Friends," September 9, 2000, http://www.willowcreek.com/store/archive_ service.asp?servid=312.

9. While usually attributed to Ralph Waldo Emerson, the saying is based on the following longer (and non-rhyming) quote from Harrington Emerson. "As to methods, there may be a million and then some, but principles are few. The man who grasps principles can successfully select his own methods. The man who tries methods, ignoring principles, is sure to have trouble," https:// twobrainbusiness.com/methods-vs-principles.

10. Andy Stanley, *Deep and Wide: Creating Churches Unchurched People Love to Attend* (Grand Rapids, MI: Zondervan, 2016), Kindle loc. 3340, (parentheses mine).

11. Francis Chan, *Letters to the Church* (Colorado Springs, CO: David C. Cook, 2018), Kindle loc. 440.

12. Brian Orme, "10 Dangerous Myths About Church Growth," Church Leaders, December 21, 2022, https://churchleaders.com/pastors/pastor-articles/164064-brian-orme-old-wives-tales-about-church-growth.html.

13. Romans 8:28.

14. Psychology Today Staff, "Toxic Positivity," *Psychology Today*, https://www.psychologytoday.com/us/basics/toxic-positivity.

15. John 16:33 NKJV.

16. Dave and Joanne Beckwith, *God Meetings: An Awakening in the Board Room* (Plymouth, MA: Elk Lake Publishing Inc., 2022), 265.

17. Thom Rainer, *The Book of Church Growth: History, Theology and Principles* (Nashville, TN: Broadman Press, 1993), 185.

18. C. Peter Wagner, *Leading Your Church to Growth* (Ventura, CA: Regal, 1984), 60.

19. Jeff Goins, *The In-Between: Embracing the Tension Between Now and the Next Big Thing* (Chicago, Moody, 2013), 21.

20. Gunner Gundersen, Tweet on 11/22/22, https://twitter.com/Gunner Gundersen/status/1595162417931354113.

21. Thomas Costello, "Get to Know Saddleback Sam—An Introduction to Rick Warren's Target Church Member," September 27, 2023, https://reachright studios.com/saddleback-sam/#h-the-origin-of-saddleback-sam.

22. Ibid.

23. Bob Smietana, *Reorganized Religion: The Reshaping of the American Church and Why It Matters* (New York: Worthy Books, 2022), Kindle 101.

24. "What Is the Ethnic Makeup of World Christianity?" FAQ page from the *Center for the Study of Global Christianity*, https://www.gordonconwell.edu/center-for-global-christianity/research/quick-facts/.

25. Howard Snyder, "Chapter 5: Renewal View," *Evaluating the Church Growth Movement: Five Views*, 62.

26. "What is the Ethnic Makeup of World Christianity?" https://www.gordon-conwell.edu/center-for-global-christianity/research/quick-facts/.

27. Smietana, *Reorganized Religion*, Kindle 103.

28. Ibid., 105.

29. Bob Smietana, "There's a Reason Every Hit Worship Song Sounds the Same," Religion News Service, April 11, 2023, https://religionnews.com/2023/04/11/theres-a-reason-every-hit-worship-song-sounds-the-same/.

30. Bob Smietana, "Big churches sound alike. Little churches are the 'Wild West' of music, study finds," Religion News Service, July 7, 2023, https://religionnews.com/2023/07/07/big-church-may-sound-alike-but-litte-churches-are-wild-west-study-finds-worship-megachurch-hymns-are-not-dead-yet/.

31. "Dunning-Kruger Effect," *Britannica*, https://www.britannica.com/science/Dunning-Kruger-effect.

32. Joyce Ehrlinger, Kerri Johnson, Matthew Banner, David Dunning, and Justin Kruger, "Why the Unskilled Are Unaware: Further Explorations of (Absent) Self-Insight Among the Incompetent," *National Library of Medicine*, January 1, 2008, https://www.ncbi.nlm.nih.gov/pmc/articles/PMC2702783/.

33. This graph is not from Dunning and Kruger's original work. I've coalesced ideas from various graphs that others have created to visualize the content of Dunning and Kruger's work. In doing so, I've used my own terms for each segment of the graph.

34. Craig Van Gelder, "Chapter 2: Gospel and Our Culture View," *Evaluating the Church Growth Movement: Five Views*, 88–89.

Chapter 10: Beyond the Big/Small Divide

Epigraph: Glenn T. Stanton, *The Myth of the Dying Church: How Christianity Is Actually Thriving in America and the World* (Brentwood, TN: Worthy Books, 2019), Kindle page 157 of 200.

1. Randall Stross, "Failing Like a Buggy Whip Maker? Better Check Your Simile," *New York Times*, Jan. 9, 2010, https://www.nytimes.com/2010/01/10/business/10digi.html.

2. Peyton Jones, *Church Plantology: The Art and Science of Planting Churches* (Grand Rapids, MI: Zondervan, 2021), 2, 6.

3. Skye Jethani, *Immeasurable: Reflections on the Soul of Ministry in the Age of Church, Inc.* Kindle loc. 718.

4. Aaron Earls, "Small Churches Continue Growing—but in Number, Not Size," October 20, 2021, https://research.lifeway.com/2021/10/20/small-churches-continue-growing-but-in-number-not-size/.

5. Tod Bolsinger, *Canoeing the Mountains: Christian Leadership In Uncharted Territory* (Downers Grove, IL: IVP Books, 2015), 118 (parentheses are Bolsinger's).

6. Seth Godin, "Measure What You Care About (Re: The Big Sign over Your Desk)," *Seth's Blog*, February 14, 2015, http://sethgodin.typepad.com/seths_blog/2015/02/measure-what-you-care-about-avoiding-the-siren-of-the-stand-in.html.

7. The original quote is "Not everything that can be counted counts. Not everything that counts can be counted." Though usually attributed to Albert Einstein, it was penned by William Bruce Cameron in his book, *Informal Sociology: A Casual Introduction to Sociological Thinking* (New York: Random House, 1963), https://quoteinvestigator.com/2010/05/26/.

8. Gregg R. Allison and Bryce Butler, *Why Transactional Leadership Hurts the Church*, The Gospel Coalition, April 4, 2022, https://www.thegospelcoalition.org/article/transactional-leadership-hurts-church/.

9. Keller's Tweets were the basis for the article "8 Reasons from Tim Keller Not to Give a Megachurch to a Single Successor," by Jessica Lea at Outreach.com, April 8, 2022. https://churchleaders.com/news/421635-tim-keller-megachurch-single-successor.html.

10. Ibid.

11. Kent and Barbara Hughes, *Liberating Ministry from the Success Syndrome*, 14.

Chapter 11: Size, Scale, and Influence

Epigraph: Terry W. Dorsett, *Mission Possible: Reaching the Next Generation through the Small Church* (Nashville, TN: Cross Books, 2012), Kindle loc. 79.

1. Carey Nieuwhof, *5 Reasons Why Engagement is the New Church Attendance*, https://careynieuwhof.com/5-reasons-why-engagement-is-the-new-church-attendance/.

2. This slogan originated in sixteenth-century France as a way for King Henry IV to express his desire for the prosperity of his people. Though often attributed wrongly to US president Herbert Hoover, it was used in 1928 by the Republican party to promote how their policies would bring prosperity to every citizen. Taegan Goddard, "Chicken In Every Pot," *Political Dictionary*, https://politicaldictionary.com/words/chicken-in-every-pot/.

3. Mark Schatzker, *The Dorito Effect: The Surprising New Truth About Food and Flavor* (New York: Simon & Schuster, 2015).

4. "The Average Chicken Weighs a Lot More than They Used To," *The Humane League*, March 31, 2021, https://thehumaneleague.org/article/average-chicken-weight.

5. "What Is the Difference between Faster- and Slower-Growing Chicken?," National Chicken Council, https://www.chickencheck.in/faq/difference-faster-slower-growing-chicken/.

6. Jeffrey M. Jones, U.S. Church Membership Falls Below Majority for First Time," Gallup, March 29, 2021, https://news.gallup.com/poll/341963/church-membership-falls-below-majority-first-time.aspx.

7. Stanton, *The Myth of the Dying Church*, Kindle loc. 400.

8. Megan Brenan, "In-Person Religious Service Attendance Is Rebounding," June 2, 2021, https://news.gallup.com/poll/350462/person-religious-service-attendance-rebounding.aspx.

9. Abby Marino, "Ed Stetzer Explains Away 'Bad Stats,' Encourages Minn. Church Leaders," Transform Minnesota, October 15, 2015, https://transformmn.org/ed-stetzer-explains-away-bad-stats-encourages-minn-church-leaders/.

10. James Lasher, "Americans Do Not Like Megachurches or Celebrity Pastors," Charisma News, May 30, 2023, https://www.charismanews.com/culture/92397-americans-do-not-like-megachurches-or-celebrity-pastors.

11. Beth Moore, in *All My Knotted-Up Life: A Memoir* (Carol Stream, IL: Tyndale, 2023), Audiobook 7:43:37, describing the first time she and her husband, Keith, went to a small(er) church, hoping to find hope and healing after experiencing a great deal of church pain.

Chapter 12: Integrity Is the New Competence

Epigraph: Katelyn Beaty, *Celebrities for Jesus: How Personas, Platforms, and Profits are Hurting the Church* (Grand Rapids, MI: Brazos Press, 2022), 161.

1. John C. Maxwell, *The 21 Indispensable Qualities of a Leader: Becoming the Person Others Will Want to Follow* (Nashville, TN: HarperCollins Leadership, 2007), xi.

2. Matthew 5:16.

3. Adam S. McHugh, *Introverts in the Church* (Downers Grove, IL: IVP Books, 2017), 155.

4. David Brooks, *The Second Mountain: The Quest for a Moral Life* (New York: Random House, 2019), audiobook 1:50:30.

5. Among the Greek words for money used elsewhere in the New Testament are *Chrema* (money: used seven times), *Ploutos* (riches, wealth: used 22 times), *Argurion* (silver money: used 20 times), and *Philarguria* (love of money, avarice: used once), https://www.biblestudytools.com/interlinear-bible/.

6. While the original meaning of *mammon* is somewhat obscure, it is widely agreed that it means greed, the drive for more, and the negative effects that this drive has on people. St. Gregory of Nyssa, St. John Chrysostom and others believed *mammon* to be a demon. "Medieval theologians assigned seven archdemons to the seven deadly sins, and Mammon became the demon of greed." Melissa Petruzzello, "Mammon," *The Encyclopaedia Brittanica*, October 12, 2023, https://www.britannica.com/topic/mammon.

7. Ryan Lokkesmoe, *Paul and His Team: What the Early Church Can Teach Us About Leadership and Influence* (Chicago: Moody, 2017), 177.

8. 1 Corinthians 10:13.

Chapter 13: Discipleship Fixes Everything

Epigraph: Peter Scazzero, *Emotionally Healthy Discipleship: Moving from Shallow Christianity to Deep Transformation* (Grand Rapids, MI: Zondervan Reflective, 2021), 21.

1. Karl Vaters, *Small Church Essentials: Field-Tested Principles for Leading a Healthy Congregation of Under 250* (Chicago: Moody, 2018), 76.

2. John S. Dickerson, *The Great Evangelical Recession: 6 Factors That Will Crash the American Church . . . and How to Prepare* (Grand Rapids, MI: Baker Books, 2013), 189.

3. Ibid., 110.

4. Holy Post podcast, Ep. 498, Interview with David Kinnaman, 1:03:30.

5. Arnold Cole and Pamela Caudill Ovwigho, "Understanding the Bible Engagement Challenge: Scientific Evidence for the Power of 4," Center for Bible Engagement, December 2009, https://bttbfiles.com/web/docs/cbe/Scientific_Evidence_for_the_Power_of_4.pdf.

Chapter 14: De-sizing the Pastor

Epigraph: Jeff Goins, *The In-Between: Embracing the Tension Between Now and the Next Big Thing* (Chicago, IL: Moody, 2013), 17.

1. Bo Lane, *Why Pastors Quit: Examining Why Pastors Quit and What We Can Do About It* (self-pub., CreateSpace, 2014), 72.

2. "38% of U.S. Pastors Have Thought About Quitting Full-Time Ministry in the Past Year," Barna, November 16, 2021, https://www.barna.com/research/pastors-well-being/.

3. Gary L. McIntosh, *The Solo Pastor: Understanding and Overcoming the Challenges of Leading a Church Alone* (Grand Rapids, MI: Baker Books, 2023), 155.

4. Glenn Packiam, *The Resilient Pastor: Leading Your Church In a Rapidly Changing World* (Grand Rapids, MI: Baker Books, 2022), 117–118.

5. Ibid., 119.

6. John Mark Comer, *The Ruthless Elimination of Hurry* (Colorado Springs, CO: WaterBrook, 2019), 3.

7. From the poem "Sermons We See" by Edgar A. Guest (1881–1959).

8. John 8:44; 10:10; 1 John 3:8; Romans 16:20; Ephesians 6:11–16; 1 Peter 5:8–9.

9. Romans 6:9; 1 Corinthians 15:24–26.

10. Philippians 4:6–7; Matthew 6:25–34.

11. Genesis 1:31; Psalm 19; Ecclesiastes 3:11; Luke 12:27; Colossians 1:16–17.

Chapter 15: De-sizing the Congregation

Epigraph: Lesslie Newbigin, *The Open Secret: An Introduction to the Theology of Mission* (Grand Rapids, MI: W. B. Eerdmans, 1978), 125.

1. "Robert Greenleaf on Servant-Leadership," Gonzaga University, *The International Journal of Servant-Leadership*, September 26, 2023, https://www.gonzaga.edu/-/media/Website/Documents/Academics/School-of-Leadership-Studies/DPLS/IJSL/Vol-1/IJSL-Vol-1-04-Greenleaf.ashx.

2. Malcolm Gladwell, *David and Goliath: Underdogs, Misfits, and the Art of Battling Giants* (New York: Hachette Books), 22–23.

3. Karl Vaters, *100 Days to a Healthier Church: A Step-By-Step Guide for Pastors and Leadership Teams* (Chicago: Moody, 2020), 37.

Chapter 16: De-sizing Evangelicalism

Epigraph: Katie Jo Ramsey, *The Lord Is My Courage: Stepping Through the Shadows of Fear Toward the Voice of Love* (Grand Rapids, MI: Zondervan reflective, 2022), Kindle loc. 394.

1. "Pando, One of the World's Largest Organisms, Is Dying," *Smithsonian Magazine*, https://www.smithsonianmag.com/smart-news/pando-one-worlds-largest-organisms-dying-180970579/.

2. Craig Van Gelder, "Chapter 2: Gospel and Our Culture View," in *Evaluating the Church Growth Movement: Five Views*, 66.

3. Dave and Joanne Beckwith, *God Meetings: An Awakening in the Board Room* (Plymouth, MA: Elk Lake Publishing Inc., 2022), 260-261 (emphasis mine).

4. From the congregational letter, *A Peek Inside Your Preacher*, by Jerry Riddle, September 8, 2011. (Shared with permission.)

5. Jim Collins and Jerry I. Porras, *Built to Last: Successful Habits of Visionary Companies (Good to Great Book 2)* (Nashville, TN: Harper Business, 2011).

6. Scot McKnight and Laura Barringer, *A Church Called Tov: Forming a Goodness Culture that Resists Abuses of Power and Promotes Healing* (Carol Stream, IL: Tyndale, 2020), 28.

7. Chuck DeGroat, *When Narcissism Comes to Church: Healing Your Community from Emotional and Spiritual Abuse* (Downers Grove, IL: IVP, 2020), 94.

8. Ibid., 104.

9. Ibid., 99.

10. Exodus 18:21; John 13:13–17; 1 Timothy 3:1–13; Titus 1:5−9.

11. Niall Ferguson, *The Square and the Tower: Networks and Power, from the Freemasons to Facebook* (Westminster, London: Penguin Press, 2018), Audiobook 13:20:45.

12. Ibid., Audiobook 13.22.30.

13. Chris Anderson, "The Long Tail," *Wired* magazine, December, Dec. 1, 2004, https://www.wired.com/2004/10/tail/.

14. Skye Jethani, "The Evangelical Industrial Complex & the Rise of Celebrity Pastors (Pt. 1)," *Christianity Today*, https://www.christianitytoday.com/pastors/2012/february-online-only/evangelical-industrial-complex-rise-of-celebrity-pastors.html.

15. Keith Green, from the article "Music or Missions?" https://lastdaysministries.com/Groups/1000086193/Last_Days_Ministries/Articles/By_Keith_Green/Music_or_Missions/Music_or_Missions.aspx.

16. Lesslie Newbigin, *The Open Secret: An Introduction to the Theology of Mission* (Grand Rapids, MI: W. B. Eerdmans, 1978), 127.

17. C. S. Lewis, *The Great Divorce* (New York: MacMillan Publishing Co., Inc., 1976), 107.

HOW CAN YOUR CHURCH GET WELL?

No church is perfect, but all churches can be healthier. If you want more for your church but aren't quite sure how to get there, *100 Days to a Healthier Church* is for you. Pastor Karl Vaters has developed a tested and proven 15-week process that's manageable, adaptable, and effective.

Also available as an eBook

Small Church Essentials is for leaders of smaller congregations. It encourages them to steward their role well, debunking myths about small churches while offering principles for leading a dynamic, healthy small church. It will help small-church leaders identify what they do well, and how to do it even better.

Also available as eBook and audiobook

MOODY
Publishers®

From the Word to Life®

A FLOURISHING PASTORAL HEARTBEAT IS POSSIBLE—FOR THOSE WHO ARE INTENTIONAL.

MOODY
Publishers®

From the Word to Life®

Ministry in modern society presents a perpetual assault on the pastor's soul. Yet far from a mournful manifesto of the burdens of pastoral life, this book is a celebration of the wonderful opportunity to shepherd God's people. In this three-part book, Schmidt unfolds an approach to sustained, joyful pastoral health.

Also available as an eBook and audiobook

When Jeff Simmons started in ministry, he was surprised at how much of his time involved business. Yet business was never a part of his theological education.

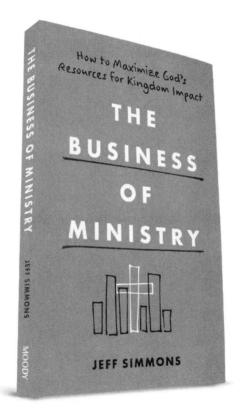

**MOODY
Publishers**

From the Word to Life

Ministries need help and guidance to become effective and wise stewards of the resources entrusted to us by God. When pastors and nonprofit leaders are good at the business side of their ministry, more people can be supported. This book helps us maximize our resources for greater kingdom impact.

Also available as an eBook and audiobook